Old Frame Chen Family
**Taijiquan**

# ✖ Old Frame Chen Family
# **Taijiquan**

Mark **Chen**

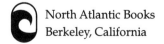

North Atlantic Books
Berkeley, California

Published by

North Atlantic Books                    Cover and book design by Brad Greene
P.O. Box 12327                          Cover calligraphy by Chen Qing Zhou
Berkeley, California 94712               Printed in Canada

*Old Frame Chen Family Taijiquan* is sponsored by the Society for the Study of Native Arts and Sciences, a nonprofit educational corporation whose goals are to develop an educational and crosscultural perspective linking various scientific, social, and artistic fields; to nurture a holistic view of arts, sciences, humanities, and healing; and to publish and distribute literature on the relationship of mind, body, and nature.

North Atlantic Books' publications are available through most bookstores. For further information, call 800-337-2665 or visit our website at www.northatlanticbooks.com.

Substantial discounts on bulk quantities are available to corporations, professional associations, and other organizations. For details and discount information, contact our special sales department.

Library of Congress Cataloging-in-Publication Data

Chen, Mark, 1964–
    Old Frame Chen family taijiquan / by Mark Chen.
        p. cm.
    Includes bibliographical references.
    ISBN 1-55643-488-X (pbk.)
    1. Tai chi. I. Title.
    GV504.C4875 2004
    613.7'148—dc22

                                                        2004000098
                                                        CIP

1 2 3 4 5 6 7 8 9 TRANS 09 08 07 06 05 04

# ✖ Contents

# Foreword

*By Master Kenneth Chung*

When the author approached me to write the foreword for his new book, I remembered the day that Master Chen Qing Zhou asked me to attend the *ru men* (discipleship) ceremony for five of his students. Master Chen distilled what could have been a complicated and overly elaborate ceremony into an event tempered with solemnity and simplicity. Similarly, in his attempt to explain Taiji, an immensely complex martial art, the author of this book succeeds with a simple approach; he communicates a rich and intricate tradition using everyday English.

I first met Mark Chen many years ago during one of Master Chen Qing Zhou's first visits to the United States. I was skeptical that someone with the author's background—that of a highly technical computer mastery—could communicate the artistic essence of Taiji as expressed by his teacher, Master Chen Qing Zhou, because Master Chen Qing Zhou did not speak any English. I have been pleasantly surprised by Mark Chen's success not only in capturing the essence of Taiji, but also in elaborating upon the concept with insight.

This book covers a broad spectrum of Taiji. Mark Chen, with his technical background, communicates the specific, physical aspects of Taiji, but he is careful also to describe it as an artistic endeavor. The Mandarin terms he uses in the book are a delight to read. English-speaking readers can simultaneously enjoy both the author's scientific understanding of Taiji and the etiquette of martial art. Since Taiji has evolved into mainstream culture, thousands of people worldwide are reaping its benefits. By practicing Taiji, one can achieve physical balance and inner peace. For those who have keen interest in the subject, but have had limited exposure to the art, this book offers the bridge between theory and practice.

# ✛ Acknowledgments

Jennifer Leech and Phil Straw saw to my care and feeding during the long months I spent hunched over my computer, and kept me going in more ways than they know.

Gwyneth Anne Freedman, Maxwell Ho, Jennifer Leech, Phil Straw, and Tony Wong all "ate bitter" for many hours under hot studio lights. I am grateful for their endurance and humor.

I am deeply indebted to Maxwell Ho and Tony Wong for assistance with numerous Chinese translations.

Without the patience, dedication, and support of Terry Chan, Daniel Gere, Maxwell Ho, Tony Mak, and Tony Wong, with whom I have spent countless hours over the years analyzing and training, this book would not have been possible.

My students at Peninsula Chen Style Taijiquan (http://www.chen. com) provided invaluable feedback in developing an instructional approach for Westerners. Every teacher aspires for one student with sufficient discipline and clarity to travel to the center of the art; I am fortunate to have several.

Grandmaster Chen Qing Zhou is among the most authoritative living sources on the subject of the Old Chen Style. His teachings and those of his sons, Masters Chen You Ze and Chen You Qiang, form the core subject matter in the pages that follow.

The manuscript for this book was prepared with L$_Y$X (http://www.lyx.org), the finest book-writing software available for love or money.

# Chapter 1

# Introduction to Taijiquan

## 1.1 What is Taijiquan?

"Taiji," people often muse, "Isn't that the thing you see old people doing in the park?"

No doubt, every vocation or avocation suffers its share of pernicious misconceptions, but Taiji seems particularly prone. In grim fascination, I once watched a television "Taiji" instructor grope his way through a joint-lock movement from a solo exercise, describing its purpose as "pushing back white, billowy clouds." These spectacles are not rare. When serious practitioners interact with the public, they often find themselves confronted by people seeking sanction for their personal Taiji religion. After one exhibition in a San Francisco community center, an audience member approached me and tried to demonstrate *kong jin* ("empty force," the ability to move objects without touching them). He made numinous gestures at me with his hands while I fidgeted in embarrassment. Whether or not *kong jin* exists, this individual certainly possessed no such skill.

As with many practices seeming mystical and Eastern, Taiji has frequently suffered cooptation by well-meaning but misinformed people hoping for a New Age panacea. It is hard to find a strip mall, health club, or Karate studio these days that does not advertise "Taiji" lessons, almost as a condition of legitimacy. The kids, they apparently reason, can beat up on each other in Karate class while the old folks do Taiji as a geriatric alternative to step aerobics. For an added bonus, practitioners will achieve harmony with the universe, improve their interpersonal skills, and cure their gout. Taiji does indeed have therapeutic properties (which are not the subject of this book), though sadly, most people will never realize them by practicing what they learn at the local New Age outlet. As for inner harmony, perhaps Taiji has something to offer, but no more than, say, playing the cello, or running triathlons, or painting murals, or doing anything else with all of one's heart and mind. Any arduous human quest teaches us about ourselves.

Taiji is not precisely about "yielding" or "softness." Consistent with common sense, Taiji avoids opposing force with force. This principle, however, is neither arcane nor unique to Taiji. Most advanced martial arts, including Jujitsu, Judo, Aikido, and Shaolin, do the same. Relaxation is indeed essential to Taiji practice, but relaxation, in Taiji terms, is not the same as softness. Taiji employs both softness and firmness as the situation demands.

Taiji is not slow. "Strip-mall" Taiji, the version that everyone has seen, is always slow because it is a tiny, sad fragment of the whole art. As with softness and firmness, any real Taiji system includes both fast and slow exercises. Of the dozen or so forms in the canon of the Old Chen Style (depending on how one counts), only two are practiced slowly. It is therefore equally accurate to say that Taiji is fast. There are logical reasons for the practice of specific exercises at specific tempi, discussed later in this book.

The word *taiji* in Chinese is often translated as "supreme ultimate." In the *Yi Jing (Book of Change)*, it is the symbol encompassing all that exists, and is the complement to *wuji*, which roughly means "formlessness."[1] *Quan* literally means "fist" but also has metonymic meanings such as "boxing," or "martial art." Taijiquan can therefore mean "all-encompassing martial art," though this makes very little sense when severed from its philosophical context. The term "Taijiquan" (used interchangeably with "Taiji" in this book) did not appear until the mid-nineteenth century, about two hundred years after the probable creation of the thing that it names. Its original name was Cannon Bashing (*pao chui*—imagine the man on TV demonstrating Cannon Bashing and talking about "white, billowy clouds"!).

Taijiquan, therefore, is first a martial art. It is, in fact, one of the most advanced martial arts of any kind, possessing some subtle properties that impart benefits to the practitioner beyond martial utility. Its superb effectiveness is a result of the fact that it teaches the practitioner to use her body and mind naturally, correctly, and with purpose. Simply that.

A person who has learned how to move correctly can move correctly all the time, whether doing Taiji or doing the dishes. She will be more effective, incur less stress physically and mentally, and generally feel better. While traditional training is quite painful and vigorous, the basics of Taiji are accessible to virtually anyone, irrespective of physical condition. This, in part, is why Taiji practice is particularly popular among the elderly. Yes, the elderly people in the park are doing (at least, *may* be doing) Taiji, but Taiji is more than what you see.

Taiji is a martial art, but there are many martial arts. What makes

Taiji *Taiji?* In abstruse, traditional fashion, I could say that Taiji uses "internal strength." This is true, but uninformative. In more descriptive terms, Taiji teaches a kind of deep coordination and *connectedness,* first with one's own body, and later with an opponent. At early stages of development, the student acquires a vocabulary of movement by training specific somatic habits. These are reinforced and refined through constant repetition until they become second nature. If studied properly, the somatic habits eventually meld into an integrated structure, so that any force applied to the structure causes instant realignment of every part. The structure shifts and adjusts in a constant flow. I call this principle "coherent movement." When one is in contact with an opponent, the opponent's structure merges with one's own. This is called *dong jin* (interpreting energy) and is perhaps the most important principle in Taiji because it entails most of the others.

When prospective students first enter a Taiji class with their baggage of misconceptions and discover that it is not at all about joyfulness or harmony or developing psychic powers, and mostly about sweating and hurting and feeling awkward, they often leave. This is unfortunate because the practice of Taijiquan is enormously fulfilling. At some point, in the midst of the sweat and the pain and the awkwardness, the student realizes that her relationship to her own body has changed dramatically.

## 1.2 The Purpose of This Book

Traditional teaching methods demand tremendous perseverance and faith from the student. Boxing masters are notorious for inflicting hardship while revealing very little about their art. This approach obviously has many serious defects, but it has one benefit. It selects the most dedicated, disciplined students and places them in an environment of discovery. The teacher creates a framework in which learning can happen; the students, in a sense, teach themselves. The learning experience is slow, but deeper and more meaningful than if lessons are handed out on a plate. The critical failing of this approach is that much of the teacher's knowledge is never actually communicated to the student. Many traditional teachers even refuse to answer questions, with the result that students lose critical details and sometimes waste a good deal of time pursuing fruitless cycles of trial and error. Students today, moreover, particularly in Western countries, are not trained from a young age and generally do not have multiple hours every day to commit to practice. What happens as a result is that they simply do not learn. Through successive generations, the art is being lost.

Unqualified instructors compound the problem by distorting lessons that they have heard or read in a book but do not fully comprehend. They will often say, "Don't use force," or "Work from the center," or even "Relax!" without any real conception of the principles underlying the aphorisms. Unless the teacher has put in years of sweat under competent supervision, ancient proverbs amount to nothing but exotic-sounding drivel. The absence of practical relevance in the curriculum is then taken as license to peddle any type of fanciful blarney, and before you know it, "don't use force" becomes "practice interpersonal harmony."

My intent, therefore, is to provide an instructional reference for the Western student who has little or no background in Chinese philosophy and cares primarily about practical results. I do not at all mean to denigrate the *Yi Jing;* it is simply that such material is not essential to the correct practice of Taiji.

There are a few responsible texts on Taijiquan in English (written by such authors as Liang Shou Yu, Douglas Wile, Robert Smith, Louis Swaim, and others), but very little on the subject of the Old Chen Style. There are also some English translations of old Chinese classics by the likes of Wu Yu Xiang, Li Yi Yu, and the Yang Family. These may be useful to advanced students, but even with a good deal of interpretive commentary, the compact, allusive writing is largely impenetrable to those who are not already expert. Alongside the tiny handful of useful texts, there is a virtual mountain of use*less* books, magazines, videos, and home-study courses, mostly produced by beginners. Let the buyer beware.

This is not a do-it-yourself manual. This is not *Taiji for Dummies*. Taiji demands a great deal of intelligence. If the reader expects immediate or easy results of any kind, I urge him to take up a different hobby. Real Taiji is an extremely subtle art, and there is simply no way to learn it without careful supervision from a qualified teacher. Many movements, for example, happen only inside the body so that it is impossible to perceive them without actually placing one's hands on the teacher's person. And while I provide step-by-step breakdowns of various exercises, a book cannot convey the quality of movement that actually makes those exercises Taiji. Even videotape fails in this regard.

The intended audience for this book therefore consists of two groups of readers:

• Diligent students who have questions or need reference material pertinent to their practice. Students who are currently working with a teacher or who have a basic grasp of Taiji principles will be able to make use of the exercises presented here.

• Those who are curious about Taiji, either from the standpoint of martial-arts theory or because they are considering learning.

It is my hope that these readers will find in the following pages a clear exposition of many Taiji principles and techniques, including material that has never before been published in English.

This is, in short, the book that I wished I had when I started learning Taijiquan.

# The Evolution of Taijiquan

## 2.1 Myth

Popular mythology attributes the creation of Taijiquan to a Daoist alchemist named Zhang San Feng (variously reported to have been born in A.D. 960, A.D. 1247, and A.D. 1279). We probably owe the Zhang San Feng legend to the third Ming Emperor, Yong Le (reigned 1403–1424), who usurped the throne from his nephew, Jian Wen (reigned 1399–1402), shortly after the latter succeeded his deceased grandfather. Seeking to foreclose the possibility of a counterrevolution, Yong Le sent out soldiers to find and assassinate his deposed predecessor. Since it would have been untoward to announce his intention to kill the rightful heir to the throne, the new emperor publicized a cover story that his soldiers were seeking the Daoist sage Zhang San Feng. News of the search spread throughout the empire. Many years later, when Jian Wen had still not been found, Yong Le consummated his fraud by erecting a monument to Zhang San Feng on Wu Dang Mountain.

No record prior to the Qing dynasty indicates that Zhang San Feng practiced martial arts. The earliest mention of Zhang San Feng as a martial artist is in Huang Zong Xi's "Epitaph for Wang Zheng Nan" (1669):[1]

> The Internal School [Neijiaquan] originated with Zhang San Feng
> of the Song dynasty. San Feng was a Daoist immortality seeker of
> the Wu Dang Mountains. Emperor Hui Zong summoned him, but
> the roads were impassable and he could not proceed. That night in
> a dream he received a martial art from the God of War and the next
> morning singlehandedly killed more than a hundred bandits.[2]

The "Epitaph" was not intended to be read as history. It is a political allegory obliquely deprecating the ruling Manchu government by holding up a well-known native Daoist (Zhang San Feng) as the originator of a superior ("internal") type of martial art in opposition to the foreign ("external," Buddhist) art practiced at Shaolin Temple. Nowhere is Taijiquan mentioned.

The first recorded reference to Zhang San Feng as originator of Taijiquan occurs about two hundred years later, in the Ma Tong Wen edition (1867) of Li Yi Yu's (1832–1892) "Short Preface" to the Taijiquan classics assembled by Wu Yu Xiang (1812–1880) and his brothers.[3] Significantly, Li's 1881 redaction of the same text omits any mention of Zhang San Feng, instead saying that "The creator of Taijiquan is unknown." The recently published "Postscript" of Wu Cheng Qing (Wu Yu Xiang's oldest brother, born c. 1800) also makes no mention of Zhang San Feng. It is probable that Yu Xiang, lacking reliable information concerning his Taijiquan lineage, concocted the Zhang San Feng story and supplied it to his student, Li. Li faithfully reproduced this story in 1867, but by 1881, one year after his teacher's death, felt freer to express his skepticism.

Why, then, would Wu Yu Xiang invent a lineage originating with this particular semi-mythical Daoist? Wu lived at a time when China's last dynasty was crumbling under commercial and political encroachments of western "barbarians." Huang Zong Xi had previously used Zhang as a symbol for rallying national sentiment against foreign invaders, and Wu Yu Xiang was clearly doing the same. Stories of Zhang were well known in Yu Xiang's time. Li Xi Yue's (c. 1800–1860) *Complete Works of Zhang San Feng* was published in 1844, recounting the Neijiaquan lineage given in Huang's "Epitaph." Li Xi Yue's work appeared just a few years before Yu Xiang's alleged visit to Wu Yang, where Cheng Qing "discovered" what was to become the textual core of the Taijiquan classics in a salt shop.[4] Interestingly, the *Wu Yang County Chronicle* contains the following entry:

> The "Cave of the Immortal Zhang" at West Pass is traditionally regarded as the site where San Feng realized immortality. The *Fu Gou Gazetteer* says that the people of Fu Gou believe Zhang San Feng left his body in the Taiji [referring here to the cosmological symbol, not the boxing method] Temple on the Wu Dang Mountains. An image of him may still be seen there. He wore a copper cymbal as a straw hat, which he allowed the people of Fu Gou to strike without becoming angry, for he was very good-natured. The people of Wu Yang also believe that San Feng was a native of Wu Yang and that they have the exclusive privilege of striking his hat.[5]

Yu Xiang probably heard many such stories from Cheng Qing, who was magistrate in Wu Yang, and whose biography records an interest in "Daoist occultism."

Writers from the Yang, Big Wu, and "Wu Dang" styles have often used the Zhang San Feng story as a way to apotheosize their own Taijiquan lineages. Yang Lu Chan himself (1799–1872, founder of the Yang Style) probably heard the story from Wu Yu Xiang, who was his student. Xu Long Hou, a student of Yang Jian Hou (1839–1917, son of Lu Chan), repeats the Zhang San Feng myth in his *Illustrated Explanation of Taijiquan Forms* (1921). He also introduces some apparently deliberate legerdemain of his own, notably the substitution of the Qing-era Wang Zong Yue (alleged author of the "Treatise on Taijiquan") for the Ming-era Wang Zong (listed in the Neijiaquan lineage in Huang Zong Xi's "Epitaph"). This bit of revisionism served to splice the Neijiaquan lineage onto the Taijiquan lineage, thus cementing Zhang's role as creator. In his *Questions and Answers on T'ai Chi Ch'uan* (1929), the Yang stylist Chen Wei Ming concedes that Wang Zong Yue and Wang Zong are different people, but then goes on to attribute some of Wu Yu Xiang's writings to Wang Zong Yue.[6] Many writers since then have attributed Wu's works to Zhang San Feng.[7] Zhang, of course, never wrote about Taijiquan or any other martial art.

Xu Long Hou's *Illustrated Explanation* was the first widely read book on the subject of Taijiquan. Since its publication, Zhang apologists have used its example to place the figure of Wang Zong Yue in widely diverse historical epochs ranging from the Song dynasty to the Qing. Analysis of the Wu, Li, and Yang family writings does suggest a common textual antecedent to the Taijiquan classics, though there exists no evidence (except Wu's salt shop story) connecting this antecedent to any Wang Zong Yue.[8] We do, however, possess an authentic martial-arts manual written by Qing scholar Chang Nai Zhou, founder of the Zhang Jia style of boxing.[9] Chang's manual bears striking resemblance to the Taijiquan classics, including many verbatim parallels. It is possible that Wu Yu Xiang created the classics based on Chang's writings and the teachings he received from Yang Lu Chan and Chen Qing Ping (Chen

Village fifteenth generation, 1795–1868); that either the salt shop manuscript or Chang borrowed from the other; or that the two were based on a third, older corpus.

By relocating Wang Zong Yue to the Ming dynasty, Xu Long Hou's *Illustrated Explanation* is indirectly responsible for another persistent myth, namely, that Wang Zong Yue taught Taijiquan to Jiang Fa, and that Jiang Fa taught it to the Chens.[10] According to Chen villagers, Jiang Fa was a rebel military officer of the late Ming who took refuge in the home of Chen Wang Ting after a failed coup attempt, and subsequently became his student. A painting above the Chen family altar depicts Chen Wang Ting seated in front of another man holding a glaive (an arrangement suggesting that the latter is a student or retainer). Villagers claim that the man holding the glaive is Jiang Fa. There is no other evidence of Jiang Fa's existence. Yang stylists since Xu's time have used *Illustrated Explanation* to claim that Jiang Fa was Chen's teacher, not his student.

To this day, there are still authors attributing the origin of Taijiquan to the Zhang San Feng/Wang Zong Yue/Jiang Fa nexus, despite a total lack of credible primary sources. In *Wu Style Taijiquan: Ancient Chinese Way to Health* (2002), Wen Zee (Big Wu Style, student of Ma Yue Liang) refreshes the Zhang San Feng myth by carefully maneuvering around some inconveniences presented by modern scholarship. He begins by commenting on the similarity between General Qi Ji Guang's "Boxing Classic: Essentials for Victory" from the *New Book of Effective Discipline* (see section 2.2) and the Yang Style long form as depicted in Xu Long Hou's *Illustrated Explanation*.[11] Reading this, one wonders why the author does not instead make the much more relevant comparison between Qi's work and the Chen Village boxing manuals, probably written about 250 years earlier than *Illustrated Explanation*, and clearly based on Qi. Yang Style descended from Chen Style, so it is rather odd to mention Qi's influence without mentioning the thing that it influenced. We discover the reason for Zee's small subterfuge a few pages later when he presents the familiar Jiang Fa story as fact, accompanied by the following emollient:[12]

- "In the 1900s, stories about Jiang Fa were popular among the elders in Beijing."

- In 1991 some Zhao Bao villagers claimed at a conference that their art was imparted by Jiang Fa.

- Modern Yang stylists say that Jiang Fa taught Taiji to the Chens.

He further implies that since the term "Taijiquan" does not appear until Wang Zong Yue's "Treatise on Taijiquan," the art cannot have existed prior to the Qing dynasty.[13] Here, now, Zee's dilemma becomes clear. He wants to marginalize the historical role of the Chens by asserting that Taijiquan did not exist before the middle of the Qing dynasty when it was "integrated" by Wang Zong Yue and passed to Jiang Fa, who, in turn, passed it to Chen Chang Xing of Chen Village. It would be rather difficult to maintain this claim in the face of authentic documents from the late Ming or early Qing (namely, the Chen Village manuals) detailing a martial art that is clearly the ancestor of the Yang and Wu styles of Taijiquan. He therefore chooses simply not to mention it, and instead uses Xu's book for the comparison to Qi Ji Guang. Zee concludes by proclaiming that Zhang San Feng is the "grandmaster" of Taijiquan because the Yang family says so,[14] in spite of his earlier admission that Zhang San Feng "was not a famous martial artist"[15] (it would, of course, be more accurate to say that Zhang San Feng was not a martial artist).

Unfortunately, the rigor of Zee's "history" is by no means below par with respect to the mass of published Taijiquan literature. While spurious texts are too numerous to list, they all inherit from the same set of sources referenced in this section.

## 2.2 History

Near the beginning of the Ming dynasty (1368–1644), the imperial government instituted a program of migrations in order to repopulate areas of the country that had been decimated by wars. One of these migrants was Chen Bu, a native of Shanxi, who settled in a small village in Wen County, Henan Province. Chen Bu's family grew large, and the village was eventually named Chen Village (*Chen Jia Gou*). Chen Bu started a martial arts school near his adopted home, but what he taught there is no longer known.

Eight generations later, Chen Wang Ting (1600–1680), ninth generation of the Chen family in Chen Village and commander of the imperial garrison force in Wen County, wrote:[16]

> Recalling past years, how bravely I fought to wipe out enemy troops, and what risks I went through! All the favours bestowed on me are now in vain! Now old and feeble, I am accompanied only by the book of "Huang Ting." Life consists in creating actions of boxing when feeling depressed, doing field work when the season comes, and spending the leisure time teaching disciples and children so that they can be worthy members of the society.[17]

The *Genealogy of the Chen Family of Chen Village* contains the following entry for Chen Wang Ting:

> Wangting, alias Zhouting, was a knight at the end of the Ming Dynasty and a scholar in the early days of the Qing Dynasty. Known in Shandong Province as a master of martial arts defeating once more than 1,000 "bandits," was originator of the bare-handed and armed combat boxing of the Chen school.[18]

Works attributed to Chen Wang Ting include the "Five Sets of Shadow Boxing," the "One Set of Long Boxing" containing 108 forms, and the "One Set of Cannon-Bashing Combat Boxing."

General Qi Ji Guang's "Boxing Classic" from his *New Book of Effective Discipline* (written in the mid-sixteenth century) lists sixteen empty-handed martial arts from all over China. Qi synthesized what he considered to be the best elements of these systems into a set of thirty-two postures, which comprise the main subject matter of the "Classic." Historian Tang Hao concluded from his researches in the 1930s that Chen Wang Ting had created Taijiquan based on this document. Tang adduces the following evidence in support of his conclusion:

- Chen's forms in aggregate contain twenty-nine of Qi's thirty-two postures.[19]

- Qi's form and all seven of Chen's forms commence with the postures Lazily Belting Clothes and Single Whip.

- The words of Chen's "Song of the Canon of Boxing" were copied from Qi's "Boxing Classic."

Contrary to Tang, historian Xu Zhen believed that Chen's Taiji was based primarily on Shaolin Taizu Long Boxing, one of the sixteen systems catalogued by Qi. Tang discounted this view because, he argued, it would mean that twenty-nine of Qi's thirty-two postures (i.e., those found in Taijiquan) were taken from Taizu Long Boxing, and only three from the other fifteen systems that Qi analyzed.

In fact, Shaolin Taizu Long Boxing, Shaolin Major Hong Boxing, Shaolin Cannon Fist, and the two empty-hand routines of Old Frame Chen Family Taijiquan all show marked similarities in form names, individual postures, and (perhaps most significantly) general choreography. Some postures from these Shaolin forms appear in Chen Taiji, but not in Qi's thirty-two. I have seen one Taizu form whose general choreography is substantially the same as Chen Taiji's First Form, and T. Dufresne and J. Nguyen cite a Shaolin form called Xinyi Boxing (not to be confused with Xingyi) bearing similar correspondence.[20]

All of this suggests that the Chen Family art was originally acquired from Shaolin Temple (a mere two-day walk from Chen Village) and later modified by Chen Wang Ting according to his reading of Qi's "Classic." Given the history of martial arts in Chen Village going all the way back to Chen Bu, it is highly unlikely that Wang Ting would have made a total break with the tradition of his ancestors by developing a boxing system from scratch (or based solely on Qi's book). The correspondence that Tang found between Qi's thirty-two and the Chen Wang Ting corpus is real, but Qi's influence was probably layered on top of a pre-existing set that had inherited from Long Boxing (or a common antecedent) before Wang Ting's time.

The question of forms, however, is only part of the larger question of Taijiquan's origin. As discussed previously, Taijiquan is defined not by techniques, but by its use of body mechanics and principles of connecting with an opponent. We glimpse some of these in the "Liang Yi Hall" manuscript attributed to Chen Wang Ting:

> As I release, bend or stretch, the opponent does not know me, leaning and coiling at will.... Everyone knows how to throw and block the enemy, but few people know how to gain the advantage through surprise. Who says I must lose when I retreat. I will lure the opponent and launch an attack to ensure my victory.[21]

Taiji principles, however, can be found in military works predating Chen Wang Ting. Wu Yu Xiang's "My opponent is still, I am still; my opponent moves, I move first" from the "Mental Elucidation of the Thirteen Postures" (1867) is an echo of Sun Zi's "I allow the enemy to initiate the attack, but my blow lands first" from the *Art of War* (Warring States period, 480–221 B.C.). In Sun Zi we also find "... avoid the enemy's fullness and attack his emptiness." In the *Wei Liao Zi* (Qin dynasty, 221–207 B.C.): "An army gains victory through stillness." And in the *San Lue* (Northern Song dynasty, A.D. 960–1127): "Softness can control hardness; weakness can control strength."

Closer to Chen Wang Ting's time, General Yu Da You (Qi Ji Guang's comrade and probable originator of the Taiji staff form) introduces the concept of sticking *(nian)* in his *Classic of Swordsmanship*. This work also contains the words "Hard prior to the opponent's force, pliancy takes advantage after his force." Another of Qi's contemporaries, Tang Shun Zhi, writes in his "Song of the Omei Daoist's Martial Art": "Giving free expression to his energy, hands grew from his entire body." This prefigures Li Yi Yu's "The whole body is as one unbroken energy.... My entire body is hands," written three centuries later. In fact, core principles of "internal" martial arts are found in every significant Ming- and Qing-era manual including Cheng Zong You's *Elucidation of Shaolin Staff Methods* (c. 1621), Wu Shu's *Record of the Arm* (c. 1662), and Zhang Kong Zhao's *Boxing Classic: Essentials of Boxing* (c. 1789). The use of both "hard" and "soft" techniques is indeed central to Chinese martial-arts theory and exists in both Taiji and Shaolin. In *Record of the Arm* we find "Shaolin excels at combining hard and soft and never tries to overcome an opponent with brute force."[22] Taijiquan, therefore, should not be regarded as a reversal of pre-existing martial principles (as Huang Zong Xi said of Neijiaquan), but a refinement of them.The earliest known authentic work embodying a substantial exposition of Taiji concepts is Chang Nai Zhou's *Writings on Martial Arts* from the Qian Long period of the Qing dynasty. Although it is entirely possible that Chang was familiar with the art practiced in Chen Village (located in Wen County, immediately adjacent to Chang's native Si Shui County), his form bears no resemblance to any known style of Taijiquan.[23] His principles, however, are nearly identical. We find discussions of connecting and sticking, neutralization, *qi* circulation, relaxation, intention, and timing—often using the same language as the Taijiquan classics. Until discovery of further evidence, it is impossible to determine whether Chang learned from the Chens, the Chens learned from Chang, or both learned from a common source.

## 2.3 The Chen Family Old Frame

Of the original seven empty-hand sets recorded in the Chen Village manuals, two remained and were taught by the fourteenth-generation successor, Chen Chang Xing. Chen villagers assert that Chang Xing unified Chen Wang Ting's routines into a single long set (First Form) and a single set of Cannon Bashing (Second Form). This may be true, but it is equally possible that the First Form is descended from Wang Ting's Thirteen Postures, the Second Form is Cannon Bashing, and the remaining five were simply lost somewhere in the five generations between Wang Ting and Chang Xing.

Most modern exponents of the Old Frame practice the system that was handed down by the eighteenth-generation successor, Chen Zhao Pei (1893–1972). This system includes Old Frame First Form, Old Frame Second Form *(pao chui)*, Taiji Single Sword, Taiji Double Sword, Taiji Single Saber, Taiji Double Saber, Spring-Autumn Waning Moon Glaive, "Five Tigers Swarming Sheep" Staff *(wu hu qun yang gun)*, Three-Opponent Staff, Pear Blossom Spear/White Ape Staff *(li hua qiang jia bai yuan gun)*, the five push-hands techniques of Chen Village, Taiji Sphere, Taiji Ruler *(xing gong bang)*, pole shaking *(dou gun zi)*, and joint locking and grappling *(na fa)*. The empty-hand forms contain the essence of Chen Family Taijiquan: silk-reeling energy *(chan si jin)*, redirection *(yin jin lou kong)*, neutralization *(zhou hua)*, locking and grappling *(na fa)*, the basic energies, etc. Weapons are used specifically for building up explosive force *(fa jin)*, sensitivity *(ling ji)*, and improving footwork.

In addition to the traditional Old Frame exercises, modern practitioners often include standing meditation *(zhan zhuang*; see section 4.9) and silk-reeling exercises *(chan si gong*; see section 4.10) in their regimen. Silk reeling was introduced in the New Frame and consists of repeated single-movement drills taken from the solo forms.

# 2.4 Other Styles

In addition to the Old Frame, there are several distinct styles within the Chen Style itself. These include:

- New Frame *(xin jia)*. This is the style developed by the seventeenth-generation successor, Chen Fa Ke (1887–1957), and propagated by his third son, Chen Zhao Kui (1928–1981). Chen Fa Ke feared that Taiji was being lost because its properties were too subtle. He therefore modified the Old Frame forms so that internal movements were accompanied by visible external movements. For this reason, New Frame forms contain more circles and are generally more ornate than their Old Frame counterparts.

- Small Frame *(xiao jia* or *Zhao Bao jia)*. This system was developed by the fourteenth-generation master Chen You Ben, and used to be called *xin jia* (before the development of what is now called *xin jia*). The general choreography is similar to Old Frame, but the movements are smaller and do not include some of the more vigorous techniques such as leaping and issuing.

- *Chen shi xin yi hun yuan* Taijiquan. This is the system developed by Feng Zhi Qiang (1926– ). Some people still call it *xin jia*, though the resemblance has grown increasingly remote over time. Feng studied with Chen Fa Ke in Beijing and is his most accomplished living disciple. Feng's system is a very complex mixture of Chen Style New Frame, Tongbei, Xingyi, and breathing exercises *(qi gong)*. It includes several empty-hand forms, straight sword, saber, ruler, and spear. The system is designed to emphasize health promotion, though some of Feng's senior students (notably, Chen Xiang) are martial artists of the highest caliber.

Before the early nineteenth century, Taijiquan was taught only within the Chen family of Chen Village. The first well-known outsider to learn Taijiquan was Yang Lu Chan (1799–1873), who worked as a servant in the household of Chen Chang Xing. According to legend, Yang evaded the village's proscription against teaching outsiders by spying on Chen's classes, and learned so well that he was later able to defeat Chen's students. When Chen saw this, he agreed to teach him. Yang eventually returned to his home in Guang Ping city, where Wu Yu Xiang and his brothers were among his students. With the help of Wu's middle brother, Wu Ru Qing, Yang acquired positions teaching martial arts to the imperial family and the imperial banner battalion in Beijing. What he taught there was probably a modified version of the Chen Family Old Frame, possibly in deference to Chen Chang Xing's proscription against teaching outsiders. The Yang style of Taiji widely practiced today is the system that was passed on by Yang Lu Chan's grandson, Yang Cheng Fu (1883–1935). This style is characterized by simple, even movements without speed changes, stomping, leaps, or *fa jin*. Two major branches of the Yang lineage are the Dong school (after Yang Cheng Fu's top disciple, Dong Ying Jie) and the Cheng Man Qing school. Yang Style is by far the most popular Taiji style practiced worldwide.

Big Wu Style Taiji was developed by Wu Quan You (1832–1902) and modified by his son, Wu Jian Quan (1870–1942).[24] Quan You was a student of Yang Lu Chan's son, Yang Ban Hou.[25] Big Wu Style is similar to Yang Style and is second to Yang Style in popularity. Until his death in 1998 at age 98, Ma Yue Liang was a leading proponent of Big Wu Style in China. His many students continue to teach in China and abroad.

Small Wu Style (also called "Li Style" or "Hao Style" after successive masters who named the system for themselves) was originally developed by Wu Yu Xiang (no relation to Wu Jian Quan). Wu studied under Yang Lu Chan during the latter's stay in Guang Ping. Deeply impressed with Yang's skill (and, perhaps, dismayed by his stinginess), he set off toward Chen Village with the intention of studying under Yang's teacher, Chen Chang Xing. On the way, he stopped in the village of Zhao Bao and met Chen Qing Ping. Wu never made it to Chen Village, but instead stayed about a month in Zhao Bao village and learned the Small Frame that had been passed to Chen Qing Ping by his teacher, Chen You Ben. Wu later combined the Small Frame with Yang Lu Chan's form to create the Small Wu Style of Taijiquan. Small Wu Style is characterized by compact postures and high stances.

Sun Style was developed by Sun Lu Tang (1860–1933), student of Hao Wei Zhen (Small Wu Style, 1849–1920). Sun was an accomplished martial artist and had achieved a high level of skill in both Xingyi and Bagua by the time he began studying Taijiquan. According to Sun's daughter, Sun Jian Yun, Sun Style incorporates Bagua's footwork, Xingyi's leg and waist techniques, and Taiji's "softness." Its appearance is similar to Yang Style, but with smaller postures and higher stances.

✖ Chapter 3

# Instruction

## 3.1 Teachers

I teach Taiji, but when people tell me that they are interested in learning a martial art, I often recommend Judo. There are various reasons for this. First, Judo is practical and effective, and it can be employed realistically after only a moderate amount of training. Second, one has a reasonable chance of locating a qualified Judo instructor in many regions of the world. Judo grades are only awarded in competition, and while competitions are certainly not the best indicator of an instructor's ability, they are at least better than credentials awarded for breaking durable objects with one's hands or performing attractive forms.

Proper Taiji instruction is, unfortunately, harder to find. Few competent instructors exist outside China, and for the novice, they can be hard to distinguish against a background of chicaners and New Age hucksters. There certainly is such a thing as Taiji credentials (I have several of them), but—putting the matter diplomatically—they mean nothing; schools hand out credentials as marketing collateral. How, then, is the avid student to go about finding a teacher?

The first step is to make sure that Taiji is what you want to learn. If you are seeking to learn a martial art strictly for self-defense purposes, Judo and Wing Chun (to name two examples) are both highly effective and offer a fairly direct route to practical results. You will, moreover, get a good physical workout and develop social connections with like-minded people. Any difference in martial efficacy between Taiji and these other arts is likely never to matter in your lifetime. I know of no one who has been mugged by a Wing Chun expert.

If you are strictly interested in exercise and health, then Taiji certainly offers some meaningful benefits. It is excellent aerobic (yes, *aerobic*) exercise and presents very little risk of injury if practiced correctly. On the other hand, Taiji is not the sort of exercise that you do with headphones on at the gym. It is not a diversion, and it is absolutely not "relaxing" (a favorite injunction of traditional teachers is *chi ku:* "eat bitter"). It is, on the contrary, physically demanding while requiring that you be completely present and attentive at all times.

Students who succeed in Taiji are generally those who are seeking a deeper relationship to their own body. Some have suffered injuries, perhaps while practicing other martial arts, and suspect that their use of their body has in some basic way been less than correct; others simply believe that they have greater physical potential and want a way to find it; and there are, of course, those who aim to acquire a pure martial art and are not afraid of the extraordinary effort and time required to achieve this through Taiji. If you are in one of these categories, then you should set about your quest armed with at least a few bits of knowledge.

As a beginner, it is unfortunately quite difficult to appraise the level of an instructor's skill by watching her perform or teach. This presents a "catch-22" to the prospective student: you need skill to identify a good teacher, and you need a teacher to develop skill. Many earnest students waste years under instructors who know nothing about Taiji.

When evaluating instructors, it is therefore useful to consider carefully three issues:

1.  Has the instructor himself been correctly trained? He need not be a grandmaster, but he must have a firm comprehension of Taiji principles. Here are some clues that will help you determine if this is the case:

    *   How much of the class is occupied by things unrelated to Taiji? If a lot of class time is devoted to discussions of joy and harmony, or if students perform their exercises to the sounds of ocean waves piped through stereo speakers, then this is probably not a real Taiji class.

    *   Does the teacher speak concretely about body mechanics, and does she demonstrate what she explains? In particular, are principles tied to applications, and does the teacher demonstrate these applications to (on) the students? One benefit of being a fake "Taiji" teacher is that your assertions are never tested. Real Taiji teachers are eager to demonstrate exactly how and why any given principle is important. Note, however, that while the willingness to demonstrate is a good sign, the teacher's ability to defeat her students means very little. For various psychological reasons, teachers almost always defeat their students, even when the students are more skilled.

- Is the curriculum complete? All legitimate Taiji styles include empty-hand forms, weapons forms, combat (push-hands) exercises, and a variety of conditioning exercises. If a teacher lacks any of these, then either his training is incomplete or he is doing something other than Taiji. It is not essential that an instructor be schooled in the complete system (even some grandmasters are not), but the curriculum should include some training in each of the cited categories.

2. Is the instructor capable of imparting his knowledge? Given the choice between studying under a grandmaster who never answers questions and studying under a thoroughly competent but less-skilled instructor with a gift for teaching, you should undoubtedly choose the latter. It will take a good, long time (possibly a lifetime) to exhaust the competent instructor's knowledge, and you will acquire that knowledge much faster and more completely than you would under the recalcitrant grandmaster. Many persistent puzzles have been solved for me by teachers only a little more skilled than I, in part due to their willingness to engage topics at a more basic level.

   Pedagogical ability is fortunately easier to assess than Taiji ability. A good Taiji teacher will possess the same traits as a good teacher in any other field. He will always answer questions and will strive for maximum clarity on every issue. It is true that Taiji perforce employs a certain amount of specialized language, but this language should be used to explain, not obfuscate. Do the students evince a common basis of understanding, or does the teacher's lengthy diatribe on "*qi* circulation" leave them with blank faces? Needless to say, any lecture that seems *deliberately* obscure or mystical bodes poorly.

3. Does the instructor have motives that conflict with yours? Some otherwise capable instructors are intractable because their objectives within the student-teacher relationship pertain to something other than imparting Taiji knowledge. Taiji instructors need to make a living like anyone else, but mercenary ambitions should not interfere with your lesson. You have a right to your teacher's best effort in every single session, irrespective of the price that you paid for it. Do not waste time with a teacher who strings you along or withholds information in order to sell more "product."

While some egregious cases of Taiji fakery can be spotted by peering at the school's brochure from across the street in a dense fog, it will generally be necessary to observe more than one class session to make a reliable assessment. You should take your time and do this.

## 3.2 "Superhuman" Feats

Bruce Lee once said, "Believe only half of what you see and definitely nothing that you hear."

If you observe enough martial-arts classes, you will eventually witness demonstrations of some apparently extraordinary feats. Some of these may be real; most are not.

There can be no question that human potential is grander than we conventionally conceive. To convince yourself of this, it is only necessary to put on a recording of Josef Hofmann or Leopold Godowsky at the piano. Setting aside issues of subjective musicality, any educated listener is forced to concede that these pianists possessed technical skills *well* beyond anything that exists today. Most music students actually consider such virtuosity impossible until they hear it. Or consider almost any aspect of the career of J.S. Bach, who once extemporized six-part counterpoint in answer to a deliberately "impossible" challenge posed by Frederick the Great of Potsdam. Douglas Adams accurately describes Bach's compositional output as "rather more than one man could actually do in a lifetime." Or consider the Parthenon, which was constructed two-and-a-half millennia ago to engineering specifications that are about an order of magnitude more precise than we can achieve with modern instruments.

The loss of certain abilities in our civilization may be at least partly blamed on our global objectivist religion: everything is a fixed, measurable quantity, including human potential. We are born with a fixed potential, and we may use that potential or not; either way, it will never change. Since we cannot build ourselves, we instead turn our energies toward building *things* to make ourselves more powerful by proxy: gadgets, weapons, corporations, etc. This peculiar religion did not exist in Bach's time. When asked on his deathbed how he had accomplished so much, Bach answered, "I worked hard. Anyone who worked as hard could achieve as much." Or in the words of *Star Trek* creator Gene Roddenberry (speaking on the "Star Trek 25th Anniversary Special" in 1991), "Ancient astronauts did not build the pyramids—human beings built them because they're clever and they work hard." So when my Taiji teacher tells me that *his* teacher was vastly more skilled than anyone around today, I suspend judgment. I cannot verify the claim; nor is there reason to believe *in principle* that it must be untrue.

With respect to most martial-arts claims, however, things that may be true in principle are almost always false in practice. In Chapter 1 I recounted a comparatively tame story about one poor truth-seeker who had convinced himself that he had learned *kong jin*. Many years ago, I visited a class taught by a husband and wife who professed to teach this technique. The students would line up and, one by one, charge full-bore across the room toward the instructor. In the midst of the student's charge, the instructor would fling out a hand. The student would stop in his tracks, then bounce energetically backward as if repelled by an unseen force, all the while making loud whooping noises. When I asked if I could try, I was told that I was not sufficiently advanced, and that the teacher's power might injure me.

There is a lesson here (besides the comic one). These students actually *believed* that they were experiencing something real. When you step into a martial-arts classroom, you are entering a complex psychological environment. Teachers in general exert a tremendous influence upon their students, and martial-arts teachers exert an implacable one. I have seen many hard-eyed objectivists completely abdicate their rationality in the face of utterly preposterous claims simply because those claims were made by a self-professed "master."

Responsible teachers do not exploit their position at the expense of their students, but even legitimate masters occasionally fall back on the odd bit of chicanery in order to please the crowd. A teacher of mine once told me a story about meeting Ma Yue Liang. Ma (unquestionably one of the most respected Taiji masters of his time) would sometimes demonstrate his power by extending his leg horizontally in front of him and allowing a volunteer to grasp under the heel and try to lift it. Ma could always press his foot back down to the ground, no matter how strong the volunteer was. The trick, my teacher explained, is to pull the foot fractionally inward at the moment the volunteer begins to lift. This unbalances him slightly and makes it impossible to continue lifting.

Some tricks are less explicit. When demonstrating combat techniques, for example, many teachers will set themselves up in a subtly advantageous position in order to ensure a decisive outcome. You should not judge this behavior too harshly. While a brief lesson from an itinerant grandmaster may seem like a small event to you, the grandmaster has a lot at stake in such an encounter. He has no idea what you might do (another of my teachers was once attacked by a seminar student in the bathroom). Even if the grandmaster's skills are hugely superior, the mere appearance of hesitation or difficulty on his part is news that will be repeated and exaggerated for the rest of his life and beyond. The small advantage that he gives himself in these situations is meager insurance against such risks.

Taiji was created at a time when people still believed in human potential. Those who practice it diligently for a lifetime can indeed do some extraordinary things, but the road to high achievement is built from very ordinary materials. No one is going to whisper a secret formula in your ear. As J.S. Bach and Gene Roddenberry both understood, you just have to work hard.

## 3.3 The Class

You compiled a list of every Taijiquan instructor within a fifty-mile radius of your home. You looked at their brochures and

Web pages and immediately dismissed eighty percent of them as bogus. You visited the rest and found one who actually might be teaching Taiji. Having observed this instructor a few times, you determined that most of her class is about movement and body mechanics; her lectures are explicit and the students seem to understand them; she evinces no sign of trying to finance her movie career with Taiji revenue; and no one is trying to do *kong jin* (whether or not it exists, it has nothing to do with Taiji).

At this point, there is nothing left but to try it out.

Chinese martial-arts classes (except the sort that substitute ritual for content) are generally conducted more informally than their Japanese counterparts. Nonetheless, if your teacher is from China, you would do well to remember a few bits of etiquette. It is common practice in the U.S. for everyone to call Chinese martial-arts teachers *shifu* (or *sifu* in Cantonese), thinking that it means "master." There are actually two forms of this word. One form is simply an honorific indicating that the honoree is a martial artist (as in "Allow me to introduce *Shifu* Jackie Chan"). The other is a form of address containing two distinct parts. The first part, *shi,* means master; the second part, *fu,* means father. This word (if we are to be strict) is properly used only by formal disciples who have undergone a certain ceremony. Normal students should instead call their teacher *laoshi,* which means "teacher" but conveys a deeper sense of respect than the English word.

If you have done martial arts in the past, you may be anxious to test your teacher's mettle and find out if this Taiji stuff is really any good; however, it is impertinent to barge into the class and throw down a gauntlet. The instructor is there to instruct, not to indulge the curiosity of arbitrary passersby. When you have participated for a while and shown your good faith, you have every right to expect firsthand demonstrations of Taiji applications (this is, after all, the point of Taiji). If they fail to materialize after several class sessions, then it is entirely appropriate to ask—*politely*, and within the context of the lesson. "What is the purpose of this movement?" is a very common and reasonable question. The instructor should be able to show you. If he or she cannot, then there may be a problem with the instructor.

When your instructor is training you in combat or using you as a "crash-test dummy" to illustrate an application, *always try your hardest* within the understood framework of the lesson (needless to say, if the instructor asks you to push his shoulder, you should not attempt a right cross instead). Due to some of the psychological factors mentioned previously, students frequently hold back against the teacher because they do not want to embarrass him or appear rude (or, perhaps, they are afraid that the mystical powers they want to believe in may not be real). This is a mistake. You are denying yourself an opportunity to learn and insulting the teacher's integrity. Qualified instructors expect your best effort at all times.

As you get to know some of your classmates, you will sometimes hear them talking about the teacher, perhaps in reverential tones. If their talk sounds *too* reverential, then this may be a bad sign. Some "teachers" encourage a cult of personality, which conflicts directly with your intention to learn Taiji. If this seems to be the case, go elsewhere. You will never learn anything here. Even in serious martial-arts classes, however, students naturally feel some degree of awe for their teacher. After all, she can clearly do some things that no one else in the class can do. The important thing to remember is that you should *never* take student testimonials at face value. Keep an open mind and judge for yourself.

The other side of this coin is that you should refrain from boasting about your teacher to other people. You yourself are biased the moment you join that class, and intelligent martial artists know this. Students who make fatuous claims in public, or habitually invoke the authority of their "master" in the presence of people who could not care less, are an embarrassment. A friend of mine who is a leading Wing Chun expert actually forbids his students from referring to him as their teacher until he explicitly gives them permission. Many instructors share this sentiment.

Finally, if your teacher is from the Old Country, you should never mention other teachers in his presence, unless he brings it up first. Many Westerners unwittingly fall into bad graces with masters from China by committing this *faux pas* ("But Master Wong says ..."). Listen, ask, and evaluate, but do not volunteer your own wisdom or contradict.

## 3.4 Your Objectives

There is a range of different emphases, even among legitimate Taiji schools. Some adhere to a strict martial-arts curriculum; others are oriented toward sporting competitions or they may emphasize health. (Even health-oriented instructors, however, should be thoroughly familiar with the martial aspects of the system.)

Competition training may seem like a good way to develop fighting skills, but generally it is not. Most competitions in the U.S. amount to shoving matches with seemingly arbitrary restrictions placed on the contestants. It is common to see a contestant cleanly throw her opponent, then be disqualified for using "too much force." Some matches restrict how the competitors may step; shuffling steps are allowed but crossing steps are not. Pushing at a small angle is allowed, but pushing at a large angle is not. And so on.

Competitions never test true skill. No matter how hard the organizers may try to create a realistic match, the competition format is artificial and the competitors know it. Good competitors usually win because they are better at exploiting the format.

Having said this, one may still regret the lack of *interesting* Taiji competition in the U.S. (there is, after all, such a thing as sport for sport's sake). Interesting Taiji competitions are just as feasible as interesting competitions in other martial arts. The Jujitsu community, for example, regularly organizes tournaments that are challenging, permit a variety of techniques, and protect the safety of the competitors.

Taiji competitions in China (such as the biennial tournament in Wen County) are less farcical than most competitions in the U.S., though they have problems of their own. The format of the Wen County tournament (where Chen Village is located) is actually similar to sumo wrestling: competitors score points by causing the opponent to step out of the ring or to touch the mat with any part of her body other than her feet. The range of Taiji skills employed in these tournaments is quite narrow, and I suspect that a sumo wrestler would dominate if one ever chose to enter. "Confrontational push-hands" tournaments with much more liberal rules existed until just a few years ago, but these were ended after a competitor was seriously injured.

Regardless of your instructor's emphasis—sport, martial art, or health—if you are not getting enough of what you need, you have three options:

1. Ask the instructor if it might be possible to make alternate arrangements. Some instructors are open to input from their students concerning class content; others are willing to supplement the curriculum with private lessons or special seminars. When you make this request, keep in mind that the answer might be "You are not ready" (particularly if your request involves combat training). This answer may well be true. Taiji training is much slower and more painstaking than most beginners expect. You should respect your teacher's judgment unless you feel that you have stopped learning.

2. Attend seminars or classes taught by other instructors. Since the 1980s, Taiji masters from China have regularly made teaching tours in Western countries. Moreover, it is often possible to arrange private or semi-private lessons while the instructor is in town. These are excellent opportunities to learn things that you can learn nowhere else.

3. If you feel that you have stopped learning and your instructor is unwilling or unable to help, then you may have no choice but to find another instructor. When this inflection point is reached by an advanced student, the easy options—i.e., (1) and (2), above—have probably been exhausted. Solving the problem therefore entails a certain life decision: how much time and energy do you want to devote to Taiji? If you are lucky enough to live in an area dense with qualified Taiji instructors (supposing such a place exists), then you can go through the entire

search process again, this time a little wiser and more discerning. Otherwise, you have two choices: practice on your own and refine what you already know; or locate another teacher, wherever he may be, and do whatever it takes to learn from him (including, perhaps, frequent trips to China and sabbaticals from work).

Finally, the issue of discipleship merits a word or two of consideration. In Chinese martial arts, a *ru men* disciple is a student who has been formally accepted by the master and has kowtowed and undertaken certain ceremonial vows of obedience and loyalty (the ritual where this all happens is called a *bai shi*).[1] It is, in principle, a two-way relationship. In return for the student's loyalty, the master agrees to teach her without holding anything back. There was logic to this relationship at one time. Before guns were widely available, skilled martial artists possessed formidable power, and teachers feared sharing this power with students who might use it in irresponsible ways.

In form, the master-disciple relationship today resembles its counterpart from centuries past, though the substance may be quite different. Since any miscreant can buy a gun, there is little concern any more (at least, from a public-safety standpoint) about evil martial artists running amok. Most teachers either teach their students well or do not; discipleship rarely provides the student with a better education than she would otherwise get by being diligent and attentive. In some cases, the disciple actually learns *less* because the teacher reasons that he has already "got" her, and does not need to do more work. There are, of course, exceptions.

Discipleship these days is mostly a political issue. Some people want the status associated with being a pedigreed lineage holder under a famous master, and their reasons may be valid. Aside from getting your name carved on a monument in Chen Village, your disciple status may help you acquire a teaching job at the local college. On the other side of the contract, many teachers regard a long list of disciples as an essential component of their resumé.

Whatever your motivations, I do not recommend considering discipleship unless you are a very advanced student and have closely observed several different teachers. I have seen many (*many*) students take discipleship vows under teachers who, they later discover, are not going to teach them anything. Once this happens, you are no longer free simply to study with someone else. Marriage may end in divorce, but discipleship is forever.

✖ Chapter 4

# Basics

## 4.1 "Internal" Martial Arts

Among Chinese martial arts, Taiji, Xingyi, and Bagua are commonly considered "internal" styles. This classification may have originated in 1894, when a group of well-known masters formed a study and training organization and called it Internal Family Boxing *(nei jia quan)*.[1] Unfortunately, the founders of the group were initially unaware of the pre-existing Neijiaquan system referenced in Huang Zong Xi's "Epitaph" (see section 2.1). They later changed the name of their organization to Internal Skill Boxing *(nei gong quan)* in order to avoid confusion, but not before many people leapt to the conclusion that these styles must all have originated on Wu Dang Mountain. In 1928 the Central Martial Arts Academy in Nanjing officially classified Taiji, Xingyi, and Bagua as "Wu Dang" systems, and since that time, the label has stuck.

Almost every martial artist considers his or her own style to be "internal," and by their own definitions, this may be true. No ecumenical definition exists (at least, none that would be broadly agreed). One common belief is that the term "internal" refers to martial arts that are "soft" or slow. By this standard, Taiji is certainly not internal since it is, on the whole, neither soft nor slow. In

────41

fact, these descriptions equally fail to encompass both Xingyi and Bagua.

Another common belief is that the term "internal" refers to the inner alchemy tradition and use of bio-energetics (*qi*). If this is true, then every Asian martial art is internal. The karateka's board-breaking, the aikidoka's "unbendable arm," the Shaolin monk's "iron shirt," the New Ager's universal harmony, and, indeed, the occultist's *kong jin* are all explained by *qi*.

Regardless of how valid this explanation may be in any particular case, the problem with *qi* theory is that it provides no common frame of reference between the student and the teacher. Telling a beginning student to move his *qi* here or there (as one frequently hears in martial-arts classes) is like telling a new-born infant to hold her own bottle; the infant simply does not know which muscles to flex, or that she has muscles at all. Students preoccupied in this way may focus on various imagined sensations (thinking them related to *qi* circulation) and consequently miss the point of their training.

In any case, distinctions between "internal" and "external" are irrelevant to the practicing martial artist. If you train with correct intent and correct body mechanics, then it makes no difference what you call your art.

# 4.2 Body Mechanics

Students who begin their Taijiquan training with backgrounds in other martial arts are often curious about what makes Taiji different from what they have done in the past. Most martial arts are defined by their techniques. When a person has learned a number of (say) Krav Maga techniques and has acquired the requisite strength and stamina to execute them, she may step onto the mat and legitimately claim to be doing "Krav Maga." A person who has similarly learned Taiji techniques cannot necessarily make the same claim.

The process of learning Taiji causes a distinct transformation in a student's perception of physical performances. Certain movements are simply "correct" from a bio-mechanical standpoint (meaning that they are executed with maximum economy and mechanical advantage), and others are not. This is true whether the movement in question is a hip throw or vacuum cleaning. After spending many years learning how to move correctly, the Taiji practitioner develops an ability to recognize correct movement in all sorts of somatic disciplines (the price to pay is the near-total loss of the ability to "suspend disbelief" while watching action movies and the like). Shaolin, for example, employs alignments that are very different from Taiji in many respects but are still correct in basic terms. Not all "martial arts" share this characteristic.

Body mechanics define Taiji movement. A person who executes a Taiji technique without using correct body mechanics is not doing Taiji. A person who uses correct body mechanics is doing Taiji regardless of the technique she uses.

## 4.3 Basic Posture and the Side Bow-Stance

When practicing Taiji, it is essential to maintain an erect back. "Erect," in this context, does not merely mean that you stand up straight. With normal posture, the abdomen is sucked in, there is a slight arch in the lower spine, and another slight arch in the neck. In order to make the entire spine (from coccyx to cranium) as straight as possible, you must relieve some of the arch in the lower back by slightly tucking in the tailbone (tilting back the hips). At the same time, lift your head as high as it will go and tuck in your chin–again, only slightly. Some teachers suggest imagining that the top of the head is suspended by a string. The classic expression for this is "Loosen the neck and lift the crown of the head" (xu ling ding jin).

Your chest should be concave. You must achieve this not by hunching (curving) the upper spine, but by allowing the shoulders to round forward a little. If you have been following my instructions, then traditional doctrine describes your present posture as "suppress the chest, pull up the back" (han xiong ba bei). This is the default posture in all styles of Taiji, though in Chen Style (Old and New), the chest actively opens and closes during certain movements. Feng Zhi Qiang's system is especially dynamic in its use of the chest.

The abdomen is discussed in detail in section 4.5 and later. For now, simply ensure that the entire region of the abdomen and the waist (including the lower back) is relaxed.

Finally, close your mouth and breathe naturally through your nose.

We will refer to the foregoing as "Basic Posture."

The Chinese word kua refers generally to the region of the pelvic bone, and specifically to the joint formed by the pelvic bone and the top of the femur (the hip joint). The expression song kua means "relax the kua" and applies to the joint supporting the weighted leg (or legs, if your stance is double-weighted). It may seem odd that you should try to relax the joint that is directly supporting most of your weight, but the reason for this will soon be made clear.

The expression "open the *kua*" means *generally* that the knees should not tip inward. In practice, this rule pertains primarily to the knee of the weighted leg, particularly in side bow-stances. It is, however, quite important to remember that all of the rules discussed in this section are applied flexibly and dynamically. In Old Chen Style the knees, including the weighted knee, frequently turn inward (thus closing the *kua*), though the open *kua* remains the default position. New Chen Style opens both hip joints more frequently than Old Chen Style (again, this will be explained later); other styles of Taiji do not use side bow-stances and consequently do not stress opening of the *kua*.

It is now time to put some of this together. Stand in Basic Posture with your heels together and your toes angled out about thirty degrees from center. Place your hands on your hips. Now shift all of your weight onto your left leg (your right heel may lift up as you do this), sink as low as you can go without tilting your torso, and slide your right foot on the inside of its heel as far as it will go to your right. As you do this, all of your weight must remain on your left leg; the inside of your right heel is just touching the ground, but the toe has not come down yet. If you feel any of your weight transferring to your right leg at this point, then you have stepped farther than you should. Once the width of your step is correct, slowly shift your weight over to your right, bending your right knee and straightening the left, and allow the right toe to come down at about a sixty-degree angle from the front. Continue to shift your weight until your right lower leg is vertical with the knee directly above the ankle and your left leg is almost straight (this may require rising up slightly). If you find that your right knee is tipping in (toward the arch of the foot), then your *kua* is not open. Open it. Once your weight is transferred to the right, turn in the toe of your left foot as far as it will go without straining. If you have done all of this correctly (I urge you to practice as much as possible in front of a mirror), you should look like figure 4.1. This is a side bow-stance, a characteristic posture of Chen Taiji.

*Figure 4.1*

It is critically important that you not straighten your left leg to such an extent that the knee locks. *Your joints should never lock;* there is no exception to this rule. Once a joint locks, that part of your body has stopped flowing and you are no longer doing Taiji. Remember (from Chapter 1) that your entire body works dynamically as an integral unit. This cannot happen if any part stops moving.

Check your posture. Make sure that you have not changed the alignment of your back in the process of shifting weight, and that your waist is relaxed. Many students (particularly office workers) have under-developed proprioception to such a degree that they do not know when they are standing straight. If you find yourself in this category, do not despair; this skill, like any other, is learned. Simply watch yourself in a mirror from the front and the side until you know what it feels like to be vertical.

Another common problem in side bow-stances is that the hips turn in the same direction as the unweighted toe. Your hips should turn neither right nor left. Their orientation should remain the same throughout this exercise.

If you have followed the directions in this section, you probably feel quite uncomfortable. This is normal. We learn—anything, not just Taiji—by repeatedly putting ourselves into an uncomfortable position until we get comfortable there. If you plan to study Taiji, you will be uncomfortable for many years, so you should accept this without becoming distressed or preoccupied.

# 4.4 Application of Basic Posture

To illustrate the practical effects of the principles discussed in the last section, we will apply those principles to a front bow-stance. You will need a partner to complete this exercise.

Our method of entering the front bow is similar to our method of entering the side bow. Stand in Basic Posture as you did previously: straighten your back, suppress your chest, relax your waist, and place your hands on your hips. Stand with your feet together and parallel. Turn the toe of your right foot out forty-five degrees, shift your weight completely to the right foot, sink as low as you can go without leaning (your left heel may lift up as you do this), and step forward with your left foot so that the heel lightly touches the ground and the ankle is relaxed (the toe of your left foot is off the ground). Front bow-stances are done at various angles; for this exercise, your left foot should be about thirty degrees left of center. Again, if there is any weight on your left foot, you have probably stepped too far. Now shift your weight forward onto the left leg as the left toe descends to the ground. Note that your torso will follow a path slightly to the left as it moves toward your left foot. Even so, your torso and your left toe should both point straight ahead (the same direction you were facing when you started), not at an angle. Your left knee should end above your left ankle, just as your right knee was above your right ankle in the previous exercise. Your right leg should be almost straight. This is a front bow-stance (figures 4.2a and 4.2b).

Figure 4.2a

Figure 4.2b

Check your posture to make sure that your right knee is not locked and you are not leaning.

Now ask your assistant to stand directly in front of you and place the palm of his hand (either hand) lightly on the center of your chest. As your assistant slowly applies pressure to your chest (just a moderate amount of pressure will do here), your job is to use your waist and hips to direct the force of his push directly through your right leg and into the ground. If you do this properly it should require very little energy. *Do not counter the push by pushing back.*

In Taiji, when a force is applied to any part of your body, you do one of two things. You either "root" it so that your opponent is effectively acting straight against the ground, or you redirect it. Redirection also implies rooting because you always use a rooted point as a fulcrum, regardless of where the force is vectored. At this moment you are simply rooting.

While your assistant continues to push with moderate pressure, violate a postural rule by arching your lower back slightly. You will immediately find that you can no longer root. Even a small arch in your lower back compromises your structural integrity by disconnecting your torso from your pelvis.

Now reset your position and have your assistant slowly increase the pressure. If you maintain correct posture, you will notice that more and more force (that is, the increased force applied by your assistant) is going into your back leg. In order to adjust to this force without resorting to muscular resistance, it becomes necessary to change slightly the angle between your right leg and the ground—to make the angle more acute (the change in this angle should be *very* small). You will also notice that any force going into your right leg reduces the amount of weight borne by your left leg. In effect, your opponent is transferring your weight into your back leg. As the angle between your right leg and the ground decreases very slightly in response to the increased pressure against your chest, you are naturally sinking deeper into your left leg (this is all simple geometry). The only way to do this is to relax the *kua*, thus allowing greater flexion between the thigh and the pelvis. If your assistant suddenly takes his hand away, you should not lunge forward; you should sink down.

Summarizing: in response to increased force, you decrease the angle between your back leg and the ground while (necessarily) sinking deeper into your front leg by relaxing your *kua*. As you do so, the weight supported by your front leg actually decreases. This is why, paradoxically, you must think of relaxing the *kua* even when doing solo exercises where most of your weight is on the front leg. You are developing a habit that will later serve you against an opponent.

Another point to notice is the fact that sinking into your front leg implies increased flexion of that knee and ankle. If you begin a bow stance with the knee too far forward (say, beyond the toe), then the process of sinking may cause you to overbalance and topple forward. This is one reason why we use a vertical lower-leg as standard in these postures.

## 4.5 The *Dan Tian* and Waist

For our purposes, the *dan tian* refers to what is actually the lower *dan tian* in Chinese medicine: a point about three fingers below the navel and about a third of the way in toward the spine. Chen Style Taiji differs from other Taiji styles in that it very actively uses the *dan tian* to initiate movements. This is unfortunately one of the most difficult points for beginners to grasp because most people have no experience of their *dan tian* whatsoever.

Expert Taiji practitioners actually have a distinct "ball" of muscle in their abdomen that they can move around at will. Their abdominal muscles in general become highly developed and elastic, resulting in power and flexibility of the waist.

Part of Chen Taiji's "basic training" consists of simple exercises designed to focus awareness on the *dan tian* and to build coordination in the internal muscles surrounding it. These are called *dan tian* rotation exercises.

Begin by standing in Basic Posture. Set your feet about shoulder-width apart with your toes pointing out at a natural angle—about fifteen or twenty degrees from center. Place the palm of your left hand on your navel and place your right hand directly below it. Completely relax your abdominal muscles so that your abdomen expands into your hands. Focus your attention particularly in the far lower abdomen. Bend your knees and sink your weight. Your posture should look like figure 4.3.

*Figure 4.3*

Now you must try to find your *dan tian*. One way to do this is to contract—*gently*—the muscles of the perineum (the sphincter and urogenital muscles) and imagine them converging to a point inside your body. Your subjective perception of that point corresponds to the location of the *dan tian*. Be certain that you do not strain as you do this. Since most people have never consciously used the muscles involved in this exercise, it is quite normal to have difficulty with this step. Consistent practice will produce results.

Once your awareness is as focused as possible, use your internal muscles to move the *dan tian* slowly in a counter-clockwise circle (clockwise relative to a person facing you) parallel to the plane of your body. The *dan tian* begins its path at the bottom of this circle, so you will start by moving to the right and up. The diameter of the circle should be about the distance from navel to diaphragm. As you move, you must coordinate three things:

- Your hands stay on the *dan tian* as it moves. In other words, they slide on your abdomen in a counter-clockwise circle.

- Your weight follows the path of your *dan tian*. As your *dan tian* moves right, your weight shifts mostly to the right leg. As your *dan tian* moves up, your legs straighten (but, as always, not all the way). As your *dan tian* moves left, your weight shifts mostly to the left leg, and as your *dan tian* returns to its origin, you sink and return your weight to center. The movement should be continuous and circular.

- You inhale as the *dan tian* moves up and exhale as it sinks.

Reverse direction after completing your third circle; that is, repeat the exercise in a clockwise direction.

As a simple demonstration of the function of the *dan tian*, set yourself up in a front bow-stance and have your assistant apply medium pressure straight to your chest. This time, rather than rooting the force, absorb some of it by slowly shifting your weight backward onto your rear leg (straightening your front leg and bending your rear leg) while maintaining correct Basic Posture. Since your stance is diagonal, the path of your torso will also be diagonal. As your assistant follows your weight shift and continues to push, you will find that somewhere between half and three-quarters of the way back (depending on how wide your stance is and several other factors), you can no longer root the force; the angle between your rear leg and the floor has become too obtuse and you are unbalanced.

Now reset and try again. This time, as you shift your weight back, simultaneously move your *dan tian* toward your spine. If you lack sufficient control to do this, simply compress your abdominal region by sucking in your stomach (a rough approximation, but one that will serve for present). If you have maintained correct posture, you will find that you can stay rooted longer than you could on the last attempt. The reason is that your *dan tian* movement has caused a subtle realignment of the muscles and bones in your lower back, and the slight change in geometry is enough to make a difference in the outcome.

An important lesson of Taiji is that minute changes in geometry can have a large effect on the overall structure and effectiveness of your body. In traditional doctrine this is called "subtle movement" *(ling dong)*. For experienced Taiji practitioners, all movements, including seemingly isolated movements of, say, the fingers, originate in the *dan tian*. You may spend a lifetime developing this ability and not reach the end of it.

## 4.6 Relaxation

The great pianists of the late Romantic era stressed to their pupils the importance of relaxation. It is quite popular these days for modern piano teachers to cluck condescendingly at those talented but naive musicians of old who, alas, did not have modern "science" to tell them that it is physically impossible to play the piano without some tension in the hand and arm. We may regard this as yet another demonstration of the human capacity for spouting complete drivel without actually telling any lies.

When we practice martial arts (and in most facets of life) we care about two things: 1) the result, and 2) the method of obtaining it. It is perfectly reasonable to stipulate (without digressing into the question of what is science and what is pseudo-scientific pablum manufactured by the medical industry) that any voluntary movement of a human body involves some sort of muscle action. This is completely true and completely irrelevant. A child does not learn to walk by analyzing which muscles must be flexed, but by imagining the sensation of walking and learning through practice to put her mind and body in that place. A chess master does not play blindfold chess by deliberately memorizing the position of every piece. As the great blindfold player George Koltanowski said, "I don't have a picture of the board in my mind. I *feel* the board, and I hear it." Thus, knowing the locations of individual pieces is merely a consequence of that larger awareness. A pianist, indeed, does not develop transcendent technique by focusing on the muscular action required to produce notes (and the question surely has some significance—who is the greater virtuoso, Leopold Godowsky concentrating on relaxation, or anyone else preaching the "scientific" need for tension?). The pianist must relax.

In Taiji we do the same; in Taiji, however, "relaxation" *(fang song)* has a very specific meaning: it is active and it is connected. Any part of your body that is completely limp is, in fact, not relaxed. Limpness usually implies a stiffness or blockage effectively disconnecting the limp part from the rest of your structure. Many beginners, when they see the quality of movement that a Taiji expert exhibits in doing forms, think that the expert is actually using a lot of force and that the concept of relaxation is more philosophical than practical. This is exactly wrong. By concentrating on *total* relaxation, you will eventually develop a sort of deep coordination that allows you to move with superb economy and cohesiveness. It is these qualities that the beginner mistakes for force.

Another consequence of relaxation is sensitivity. Stiffness, by contrast, disconnects you both from your own body and from your opponent's. The concept of "listening to the opponent's energy" *(ting jin)* means that your body is sensitive to the opponent's changes in direction and force. "Interpreting the opponent's energy" *(dong jin)* is the next level of skill; it means that any shift in the opponent's structure instantly causes a corresponding adjustment in yours. Relaxation is the prerequisite for both of these skills.

The subjective experience of correct relaxation is a feeling of aliveness and consciousness throughout your whole body. Your body feels substantial when it moves, as if possessing great inertial mass, yet movement is effortless. The *Yang Family Forty Chapters* expresses the matter in traditional enigmatic terms:

> We must first understand the meaning of the words conscious movement. After grasping conscious movement, we can begin to interpret energy, and finally, from interpreting energy, proceed to spiritual illumination. However, at the beginning of practice, we must gain an understanding of conscious movement, which, although it is part of our natural endowment, is very difficult to grasp.[2]

While certain benefits of relaxation may be easy to understand, it seems impossible that one should be able to prevail over an opponent without the application of some force. According to most Taiji schools, the process of engaging with an opponent seems to go something like this:

1. Be soft and harmonious.

2. Magic happens.

3. Opponent is defeated.

Any reasonable person should be skeptical upon hearing such news.

The important thing to understand at this stage is that relaxation is not the same as softness. Taiji employs the entire range of postural consistencies from completely empty to completely firm, as the situation demands. In section 4.4 we conducted a rudimentary exercise in "firmness" where you received a force from your opponent and used your waist and *kua* to direct it into the ground. Precise application of the same basic principle (that is, alignment of joints rather than resistance with muscle) permits you to make any part of your body as solid or as pliable as you want.

If you absorb force by vectoring it into the ground, it stands to reason that you issue force by bringing it up *from* the ground. The exact techniques for achieving this are discussed in detail in section 4.10 and in later parts of this book.

## 4.7 Stances and Foot Techniques

In a previous exercise, we used a front bow-stance in which the front foot was placed forward at about a thirty-degree angle. While this particular angle has no significance, it is important to know that the size of the angle affects your lateral stability. If the direction of an incoming force is perpendicular to the line between your feet, the force is harder to root or redirect than it would be otherwise. If your feet are parallel to the direction of force (still speaking of front bow-stances), your legs may have good mechanical advantage, but your waist has very little freedom to turn toward the weighted leg, and the axis through your feet is narrower than your hips. All of this makes you less stable. Note that in side bow-stances, your torso does not face the opponent (the axis through your shoulders is parallel to the axis through your feet), allowing more freedom to turn in the direction of the weighted leg. Side bow-stances are therefore used when the opponent is directly or almost directly to your side.

One difference between Old Chen Style and New Chen Style is the orientation of the foot (in other words, the direction that the toe points relative to the heel of the foot). As explained previously, Old Chen Style generally turns the toe of the unweighted foot slightly inward. In New Chen Style the toe of the unweighted foot turns outward in both side and front bow-stances. This allows the *kua* to open on both sides, creating the characteristic "bridge" of New Chen Style (the legs form a shape resembling an arch bridge).

The reason for this difference relates to different tactical assumptions. By having the toe of the unweighted foot point outward, the New Chen Stylist positions herself to defend against opponents who may be attacking from different angles. The open toe makes it easier to turn the waist and torso quickly toward the unweighted foot, and the arched leg provides some protection against attacks to the knee. New Chen Style is unique in this respect; no other style of Taiji uses this type of stance.

Old Chen Style's front bow-stance, by contrast, provides greater freedom to turn the torso toward the weighted leg in order to face an opponent who is standing directly in front. To illustrate, stand in a front bow-stance as described in section 4.4 and turn your waist as far as it will go in the direction of the weighted leg. If your posture is correct, the toe of your unweighted foot points forward at about a forty-five-degree angle. Now try to turn this toe out (to the right, if the right foot is unweighted, to the left otherwise). You will find that you cannot do it without changing the orientation of your torso; as the foot turns, your torso turns with it. The relationship between foot angle and waist freedom is clearly seen in movements such as Oblique Posture (see Chapter 5). Old Chen Style's version of this movement faces directly forward, whereas in New Chen Style, the torso faces slightly right to accommodate the turned-out right toe.

*The most significant consequence of foot placement and orientation is the range of movement afforded your waist.* As the back toe turns out, your waist has more freedom toward the back and less toward the front. As the angle between your front and back foot increases (that is, the angle between the axis through the feet and the direction you are facing), you gain freedom toward the front and lose it in the back. The second consequence of foot placement is stability relative to the direction of force. You gain mechanical advantage as the axis through your feet and the direction of force approach parallel and lose it as they approach perpendicular.

Any stance, therefore, is a compromise between mechanical advantage and freedom. The side bow-stance (which exists only in Chen Style) resolves this conflict by placing both the feet and the shoulders nearly in line with the opponent. By facing the opponent sideways, the torso and waist have more range on the weighted side, though the opposite hand loses its reach. For this reason, side bow-stances are often used in conjunction with shoulder and hip strikes.

A final point to consider is that in Old Chen Style, the knees and feet serve an offensive function, even while the feet remain planted on the ground. This issue is discussed in section 6.1.

## Horse Stance

This is the only stance in Taiji where the two legs bear approximately equal weight, and it occurs only rarely in forms practice. Stand in Basic Posture with your feet anywhere between shoulder-width and twice shoulder-width apart and your toes pointing out about fifteen or twenty degrees from center. Sink straight down as far as you can go without leaning, and keep your weight evenly distributed along both feet (see figure 4.4).

This stance mostly serves a transitional function wherein the weight has not yet shifted to one side or the other.

*Figure 4.4*

## Empty Stance

Stand in Basic Posture with your feet together. Turn the toe of one foot out about thirty degrees and transfer all of your weight onto that leg. Sink straight down and place the toe of the unweighted foot on the ground about shoulder width from the weighted foot and forward at a forty-five-degree angle (see figure 4.5). There should be no weight whatsoever on the unweighted foot; it just touches the ground. Note that the position of the unweighted foot varies in these

*Figure 4.5*

stances. Sometimes it is in front (as in the present example), and sometimes it is directly to the side.

Empty stances occur frequently and are usually used either as preparation for an advance or attack with the unweighted leg, or to attack an opponent on the weighted side.

Figure 4.6

## Squat Stance

Stand in a side bow-stance and squat all the way down onto one leg while keeping the back perfectly straight (see figure 4.6). The toe of the unweighted foot sometimes tips up and sometimes remains flat.

Squat stances are often used in ducking techniques and techniques where you pull the opponent low.

## Resting Stance

Stand in Basic Posture with your feet shoulder width apart. Transfer all of your weight onto one foot (we will use the right foot in this example) and step the left foot sideways across the right foot to a position about shoulder width distant on the opposite side. The toes of both feet should remain in line. Shift about sixty percent of your weight to the left foot and squat down low without leaning. As you sink, the heel of the right foot will lift off the ground while the left foot remains flat. The right knee should remain in contact with and locked behind the left knee so that you are sort of "sitting" on your right leg. The torso should not turn from its starting orientation (see figure 4.7).

Resting stances are used to advance sideways toward an opponent.

## Split Stance

The split stance is similar to the squat stance, but lower.

Begin in a squat stance and sink all the way down until you are almost (but not quite) sitting on the ground. As you sink, the toe of your unweighted foot will tip up and the foot will slide out a bit. The knee and foot on the weighted side will tip in and the knee may touch the ground, but there should be no weight on it; all of your weight remains on your feet (see figure 4.8).

*Figure 4.7*

Split stances are used in ducking techniques and techniques where you rise up to attack the opponent from below. Certain squat stances in the First Form are sometimes practiced as split stances.

*Figure 4.8*

## Weight Shifting

Earlier in this chapter, we discussed the function of the *kua* and back leg in vectoring (rooting) the opponent's force into the ground. Correct weight-shifting technique employs the same principles continuously as the weight moves from one leg to the other.

Whether the opponent is on the weighted or unweighted side of your stance, you first sink your *kua* on the weighted side in order to control the vector of his force (again, this is simple geometry). If you are already settled into a side bow-stance, this sinking action will naturally cause a slight turning of your hips and torso toward the weighted leg. Without this small turn, the increased flexion of your weighted knee causes your weight to shift farther toward (or even, perhaps, outside) the weighted foot, resulting in decreased stability. The turn effectively absorbs the extension of the unweighted leg that occurs when the angle of the leg goes slightly lower toward the ground. The correct motion is therefore a small, downward corkscrew with the hips, rather than a tilting toward the weighted leg.

As weight moves to the other side, the hips straighten out until they are once again in line with the axis of your stance. At the same time, the toe of the now-weighted foot turns out while the other toe turns in.

Some instructors and authors describe this motion as a "figure eight" (referring to the path traced by the tailbone along the ground as weight travels side to side). This is misleading because it implies deliberate front-to-back movement of the hips.

## Stepping

For reasons cited earlier in this section, forward and backward stepping in Taiji is always done at an angle. This means that if you are walking forward in an easterly direction, your steps do not land directly on an east-west line, but somewhat north or south of that line (north with the left foot, south with the right). In order to maintain balance, your feet should move in and out from your center. Thus, each step follows a slight arc: in toward the vertical axis of your body (centered over our east-west line in the present example), then out again, slightly to the side.

For example, when stepping forward from a front bow-stance, use the following procedure:

1. Stand in a front bow-stance (see figure 4.9).

2. Weight shifts completely to the front leg as the toe of the front foot turns out. Back foot travels in toward the center of the body, then forward at an angle toward the outside. The heel touches ground lightly (see figure 4.10).

3. Weight shifts to the front leg as the front toe descends to point straight forward (see figure 4.11).

*Figure 4.9*            *Figure 4.10*            *Figure 4.11*

When stepping backward:

1. Weight shifts completely to the back leg. The front toe may optionally turn in (because it is easier for the foot to step off of the toe than off of the heel; see figure 4.12).

2. Front foot travels in toward the center of the body, then backward at an angle to the outside. The toe touches ground first,

Figure 4.12

Figure 4.13

Figure 4.14

then the heel descends so that the foot points forward at an angle (see figure 4.13).

3. Weight shifts to the back leg as the front toe turns to point straight forward (see figure 4.14).

Note that the stepping foot is always placed lightly on the ground before any weight is transferred to it.[3] This serves two purposes: 1) it trains you to remain balanced while stepping, and 2) it allows you to withdraw the foot quickly if the position becomes unsafe.

## Slide-Stepping

Slide-stepping is different from basic stepping as described previously. Slide-stepping occurs in either a forward-diagonal or sideways direction.

When slide-stepping forward:

1. Stand in a front bow-stance (see figure 4.15).

2. Weight shifts completely to the front leg as the hips, torso, and front toe turn out (in the direction of the weighted leg). Back

*Figure 4.15*          *Figure 4.16*          *Figure 4.17*

foot travels in toward the center of the body, then forward at an angle toward the outside (the axis through the hips should point in the same direction as the foot's outward travel). The stepping foot passes just above the ground and may slide lightly (with the instep side of the heel touching the ground) for the last few inches of its travel (see figure 4.16).

3. Weight shifts to the front leg as the torso and front toe turn straight forward (see figure 4.17).

When slide-stepping sideways, weight sinks down, and the stepping foot travels straight to the side. The foot passes just above the ground and may slide lightly on the inside of the heel for the last few inches of its travel. Sideways slide-steps usually precede a side bow-stance. In this case, shift weight and tip the toe down into the appropriate position.

Slide-stepping is often used to close quickly with the opponent in preparation for a shoulder or hip strike. The stepping foot goes directly between the opponent's feet.

# 4.8 Hand Techniques

Taiji's hand configurations are ostensibly simple and surprisingly difficult. Students frequently have trouble maintaining correct conformation while staying properly relaxed. Uncontrolled or badly conformed hands (which afflict every beginner) are an indication that the hands are disconnected from the rest of the body's structure. These defects must be repaired while maintaining complete relaxation in the arms.

## Open Palm

Grandmaster Chen Zhao Pei was fond of explaining that the hand in Taiji should be "like a virgin." For students living in more liberated times, this means that the fingers should be held straight and close together (highly orthodox instructors may insist that the fingers actually touch, but this is not essential). The base of the thumb and the base of the fifth finger both pull in slightly toward the center of the hand so that the palm is slightly cupped (see figure 4.18). The traditional (and not very enlightening) explanation often given for this configuration is that it keeps the $qi$ in the palm. The practical explanation is that it trains your hands for joint locking: the close fingers prevent the opponent from grabbing individual digits, and the cupping creates the correct basic geometry for catching the opponent. This hand configuration is simply called "open palm" *(zhang).*

*Figure 4.18*

In certain movements (particularly upward-lifting and circling movements), the pulling-in of the thumb and fifth finger becomes slightly more pronounced. This is called "tile palm" *(wa long zhang)* because the hand resembles a curved roof tile.

## Fist

Begin with an open palm and curl the fingers tightly, beginning with the end joints and proceeding inward until the proximal phalanx bones (the finger bones closest to the palm) are about perpendicular to the metacarpals (the back of your hand). Curl the thumb over the second and third middle phalanx bones (see figure 4.19). Because the fourth and fifth fingers are shorter than the second and third, there is a natural tendency to curl them farther

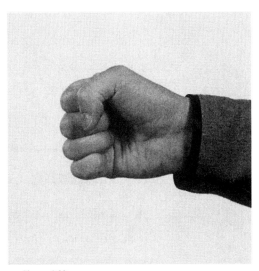

*Figure 4.19*

into the palm so that their proximal phalanx bones recede a bit from the others. Do not do this. The surface formed by all four proximal phalanx bones (the front of your fist) should be fairly flat. Your fist should be quite firm, but the arm must remain completely relaxed.

Although Old Chen Style uses the various surfaces of the fist to strike in various orientations, the shape of the fist is always the same. Newer styles of Taijiquan (notably, Feng Zhi Qiang's style) sometimes use fists in which one or more knuckles protrude.

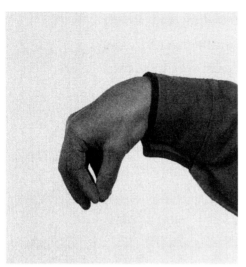

*Figure 4.20*

## Hook Hand

Bunch together the fingertips of the thumb, second, fourth, and fifth fingers. The third finger remains close to the others but with a small gap in between. The fingers point down (or sometimes up) and the wrist is completely relaxed (see figure 4.20). This is the "hook hand" *(gou shou)*.

Hook hand is often used in joint-locking techniques, especially in reversals.

# 4.9 Standing

As soon as two opponents make contact, there is an energy imbalance. One party applies a force and the other adjusts her structure to neutralize. From the first instant in which this happens, the situation is asymmetrical; some parts of the structure have more energy—are "fuller"—and others are more "empty."

The engagement therefore has two distinct phases: a *wuji* phase in which nothing has happened yet and the opponents are in balance (symmetry), and a *taiji* (small "t") phase in which they have made contact, either physically or by intention. In the *taiji* phase, there is always asymmetry; empty and full have separated and are in a continuous state of flux.

Standing meditation exercises *(zhan zhuang)*, similarly, are of two distinct types. *Wuji* standing is symmetrical and applies little or no physical stress to the body; *taiji* standing is asymmetrical and physically demanding. Both types of standing exercise use relaxation to develop connectedness and deep coordination, but *taiji* standing additionally trains the static aspects of Taijiquan body mechanics and rooting.

Almost any completed posture from a solo form may be used as a *taiji* standing exercise. The *taiji* exercise presented here is from Small Frame Chen Style *(xiao jia)*.

Begin by standing in Basic Posture with the insteps of your feet shoulder-width apart. In other words, your insteps should line up with the outsides of your shoulders. The toes of your feet should point out at a natural angle—about twenty degrees from center—and your weight is centered. Open your right hand and make the fingers completely straight and close together. Raise it so that the fingers point straight up, the tip of the middle finger is about sixteen inches in front of your nose, and the palm faces left. Focus your eyes on the tip of the middle finger. Make your left hand into a hook hand (see section 4.8) and place it behind your back at the base of your spine with the fingers pointing up. Now sink as deeply as you can go into a horse stance (see section 4.7). Your posture should look like figures 4.21a and 4.21b.

*Figure 4.21a*

*Figure 4.21b*

Also, observe the following points:

- The right elbow should be slightly "buoyant"; it should neither collapse completely downward nor stick out at an aggressive angle.

- Breathe slowly and evenly.

- Awareness should be centered on the *dan tian*.

- The sphincter and urogenital muscles should gently contract, but not to the point where it causes tension in the body.

- Eyes should be relaxed and about halfway closed.

- Weight should be evenly distributed along the length of each foot, and the toes of the feet may very gently "grip" the ground; that is, they curl down slightly.

- The whole body should be completely relaxed.

Breathing for this exercise is traditionally coordinated with mental repetition of the syllables *e, xi, xu, chui* (one syllable for each exhale or inhale, beginning with the exhale). The purpose is simply to ensure that the breathing remains even.

The first time you try this exercise, you will become acutely conscious of the fact that you never know exactly what your body is doing all at once. You will focus on the correct positioning of, say, your right hand, then discover that your back is no longer vertical; when you correct the back, you find that your left shoulder has become tense, etc. The key to success is a rule that also applies to flying an airplane on instruments: *do not fixate*. Beginners will often seize mentally on a particular problem area while the rest of their posture falters. You should avoid this error by gently shifting your focus from one place to another (without leaving the *dan tian*), making corrections as needed. Correct, move on, correct again. If you do this diligently over a period of months, you will find that your posture drifts less during each successive practice session because your awareness expands; part of your consciousness remains where you made a correction, even when the center of your attention moves elsewhere. You will eventually develop a comprehensive awareness of your entire posture so that your mind is free to focus where it will without losing track of any individual part. This is a primary objective of the exercise, and a necessary step in learning Taijiquan.

If you have been following the exercise up to this point, you are probably wondering why I have so far neglected to mention its most obvious feature: the intense, searing pain in your legs. After less than a minute, the pain may be so distracting that it seems nearly impossible to attend to correct posture. Nonetheless, you must do so. You must also hold this posture as long as you possibly can. Most students reach the breaking point at about ninety seconds on their first attempt. If you are able to do substantially more than this, then either you have a lot of prior training in Chinese martial arts or your posture is incorrect. Check that your back is vertical, your lower back is not arched, you are sunk as low as you can go, and your weight is evenly distributed across your feet. It is rather easy to cheat by violating any of these rules. You will find, for example, that leaning slightly backward shifts the stress on the leg muscles so that the whole ordeal becomes considerably easier to endure. Unfortunately, the correct posture is the one that hurts most.

If you practice this exercise two to four times a day, you will begin to see improvement very quickly—probably after a week or so. Your legs will get stronger and you will feel a bit more comfortable each time. As this happens, you must increase the duration of your practice sessions. Increments of fifteen seconds generally work well. The longer you stand, the more benefit you get from the exercise.

# 4.10 The "Energies"

The Chinese word *qi*, typically translated as "energy," actually refers to a sort of ethereal or potential energy; *qi* does not relate to the direct application of physical power. The word *jin,* also translated as "energy," refers to manifest or kinetic energy. The term "basic energies" in Taijiquan refers to the latter. To avoid confusion, we will instead use the more apt English description, "basic techniques," except when referring specifically to a quality of movement.

## Basic Techniques

Bruce Lee (returning to one of my favorite sources) once said, "… the [western] boxer … uses the basic tools of the jab, hook, cross, uppercut. … Do not let anyone tell you that martial art is different from boxing." He was mistaken about this. Boxing is not, in fact, a martial art—not because it has few techniques, but because of the assumptions it makes about the opponent. If your training assumes that the opponent will do nothing except stand at a polite distance and throw punches, if you have no way to deal with an opponent who grapples, locks, throws, bites, head-butts, strikes with shoulders, elbows, hips, knees, or feet, then you are practicing a sport (there is nothing wrong with this, of course—it is just different from a martial art). Lee was correct, however, in implying that a plethora of techniques does not a martial art make. A martial artist requires only a few techniques to be effective, as long as these techniques are sound and properly trained. Xingyi has only five basic techniques, and it is certainly a martial art. In the same sense, it can be argued that Taijiquan has eight.

The four primary techniques are:

• Lifting up *(peng)*. *Peng* expands upward and outward toward the opponent. It is a relaxed "fullness" that allows the limbs to be substantial without being stiff or losing sensitivity, and it is present to some degree in every movement. The word *peng* is often translated as "ward-off."

• Diverting *(lü)*. This is a sideways redirection of an incoming force at an angle less than ninety degrees to the original vector (in other words, part of the original force is borrowed as it is redirected). The word *lü* is often translated as "stroking" or "rollback."

• Pressing *(ji)*. *Ji* (literally, "squeezing") is a press directly into the opponent in a vector parallel to the floor.

• Pushing *(an)*. *An* is a downward push into the opponent.

The four secondary techniques are:

• Pulling down *(cai)*. *Cai* is a grab and pull toward the ground.

• Splitting *(lie)*. *Lie* is a sharp, horizontal rotation used to strike, block, or throw the opponent.

• Elbowing *(zhou)*. This is any strike with an elbow.

- Butting *(kao)*. *Kao* is usually translated as "shoulder strike," but the word can also apply to butting strikes with almost any part of the central trunk: shoulders, chest, back, and hips. Less commonly, the word is used to mean a sharp strike with any part of the body.

The foregoing eight techniques (four primary and four secondary) are basic to every Taiji style. Chen Style additionally incorporates several tertiary techniques: dodging *(shan)*, jumping *(teng)*, dissipating *(yin kong)*, throwing *(shuai)*, hitting *(da)*, and locking *(qin na)*. *Shan, teng, shuai,* and *da* are self-explanatory. *Yin kong* is the basic Taiji principle of "leading into emptiness," which simply means redirecting the opponent's attack so that it does not arrive at the target, often with the result that the opponent becomes unbalanced. This principle is closely related to neutralization *(zhou hua)* and is fully discussed in Chapter 6. *Qin na* is the method of controlling the opponent by seizing and locking his joints. It is a specialty of Chen Style.

Although these basic techniques are employed throughout the Taiji curriculum, they never appear in a "pure" form. Any movement will contain elements of more than one technique, and there is often much room for debate regarding exactly which techniques are present in a given movement. To some extent, the list seems almost arbitrary. One can ask, for example, why there is a technique named after an elbow strike, but none named after a knee strike. Indeed, different authorities will actually cite different lists. Some include "sticking and following" (*zhan, lian, nian,* and *sui*— see Chapter 6) among the basic techniques, while others include the "five phases" *(wu xing)*: advance, retreat, look left, gaze right, and central equilibrium.[4]

In some sense, the basic techniques are simply names of things that can happen in combat and do not by themselves carry much didactic power. Any martial art can claim to have techniques that go up, sideways, forward, and down. Does this mean that they are doing *peng, lü, ji,* and *an?* A purist would argue that the basic techniques are more than just techniques; they are distinct qualities of kinetic energy.

However you choose to view the matter, it is best not to over-analyze. The "basic techniques" concept provides some benefit when discussing tactics (*lü* often counters *peng, ji* often counters *lü, an* often counters *ji,* etc.), but it is of little practical value otherwise. *Correct Taiji results from correct focus and correct body mechanics.* If you practice correctly, it makes no difference whether you call any particular technique *peng* or *ji.*

## Silk-Reeling Energy

Silk-reeling energy *(chan si jin)* is the basic movement characteristic of Chen Style Taiji.[5] To an observer, *chan si jin* appears as a smooth, spiralling quality of movement. If the alignments and postural principles discussed earlier in this chapter describe Taiji's static mechanics, then *chan si jin* is what happens to these mechanics when you set them in motion. It is a result of Taiji's deep coordination and connectedness, where every joint in the body is in a continuous, coherent state of realignment in response to the ebb and flow of the opponent's force. *Chan si jin* is present in every gesture of Chen Taiji.

This principle of coherent movement is at the heart of Wu Yu Xiang's aphorism, "When one part moves, every part moves. When one part is still, every part is still."

New Chen Style's curriculum includes silk-reeling exercises *(chan si gong)*, which are simply repetitive drills taken from individual movements in the solo forms.

## Issuing

All advanced martial arts have techniques for using the body to generate more power than can be generated by the arms alone. Jeet Kune Do's method, for example, is to put the weight of the body behind the blow. The Jeet Kune Do practitioner rotates her waist and hips toward the opponent while her back foot propels her weight forward (the heel of the back foot actually lifts off the ground). The blow must reach its target before the attacker's weight transfers to the front foot so that the weight goes into the target, not into the ground. If stepping while striking, the blow lands before the stepping foot touches down.

Most martial arts use some combination of these techniques (namely, hip rotation and body weight). Western boxing does something fairly similar, as do Karate and Tae Kwon Do.

There are several problems with the Jeet Kune Do method:

- It requires a weight shift to be optimally effective. This creates an awkward situation when the front foot is already weighted.

- The attacker is not rooted when her blow lands. She may strike with great momentum, but a substantial part of the force will dissipate from recoil (a demonstration of this is described below).

- The attacking movement is highly committed. The attacker deliberately suspends her weight in transit so that it can land behind the blow. While doing this, she cannot check or alter her action. If she is very agile she can perform the maneuver quickly enough to minimize her window of vulnerability, but the window never disappears.

From the standpoint of the Taiji practitioner, however, the most basic flaw in this approach is that it does not employ coherent movement and consequently fails to muster all of the body's power. If you have carefully read the preceding sections, then it should come as no surprise that Taiji's method of power generation engages every joint in the body *simultaneously* in exactly the same way that every other Taiji movement does.

Issuing energy (*fa jin*) is simply the application of *chan si jin* to attack. It is an explosive, directed unwinding in which every joint and process in the body extends or rotates in concert toward the point of application. This happens in a rippling, whip-like motion that originates in the *dan tian* and waist and propagates at once downward into the rooted foot and out toward the target. (If you prefer, you may instead think of it as coming up from the rooted foot and out toward the target—it really makes no difference.) The waist is indeed vitally important for generating any kind of power from a human body, but, as we will see in a moment, proper use of the waist is an infinitely more subtle matter than simply turning it toward the opponent.

It is, unfortunately, impossible to learn *fa jin* from a book, but we will present here a rudimentary exercise to illustrate the basic dynamics and to provide some pointers for correct practice. For this example we will use the movement called Covered Hand Punch (*yan shou hong quan*) from the First Form.

Begin by standing in a sit stance (this is simply a front bow-stance before the weight shifts to the front foot) with your left foot forward at an angle of about forty-five degrees from center. Your left hand

Figure 4.22

Figure 4.23

extends straight ahead with its palm facing down, and your right hand makes a palm-up fist at the bottom of the right side of your rib cage. Your waist and hips are turned a moderate amount to the right, and you are looking straight ahead (see figure 4.22).

Your end posture is going to look like figure 4.23, but we must consider several issues before you get there.

One of the most evident features of this particular technique is that it is long, meaning that your hand and body travel a long distance from the beginning of the movement to the destination. Taiji has long-, medium-, and short-range techniques, but, as with most advanced martial arts, Taiji has a distinct preference for very close infighting. There are two reasons for this. First, the closer you are to the opponent, the more the outcome has to do with skill and the less it has to do with luck. Second, Taiji's principles of adhering and following (discussed in Chapter 6) are most effective in close contact. "Close," in Taiji terms, is very close indeed; your hips or torso may be touching the opponent.

*All* power in Taiji is short, whether the travel distance is short or long. When *fa jin* is delivered with a short movement, it is sometimes called "short power" *(duan jin)* or "shaking power" *(dou jin),* though the technique in every case is exactly the same. A long travel distance (as in our present example) may be traversed quickly or slowly, as appropriate; the speed of closing has little to do with how much power is delivered at the point of impact. *Fa jin* requires no wind up, no draw-back of any kind.

By contrast, the western boxer must always strike from long or medium range (western boxing, contrary to popular belief, is not close-range combat), and therefore relies entirely on speed to ensure that the target is still there when his blow arrives. He must initiate his attack with great force and exploit momentum to make it count. The boxing glove itself supports the logic of this method. Its inertial mass demands a large expenditure of energy to set it moving, but once it is moving, the inertial mass becomes kinetic energy and contributes to the force of the blow. Boxing is therefore logical within its own framework. (Taiji also has kinetic training; this is discussed in the next chapter.)

Boxing, however, is not a martial art, and techniques that work in a boxing ring may be considerably less effective when the opponent is unfettered by rules. In order to execute a long, kinetic punch, it is necessary to produce an explosion of energy at the beginning of the movement, and this energy cannot be re-applied at the point of impact (the neurons only fire once). With *fa jin,* the explosion happens virtually *at* the point of impact. Thus, the body's total power (not just momentum of the hand) is released directly into the opponent, supported by a coherent, rooted structure.

The only way to achieve this is to remain totally relaxed. Pay particular attention to your right hand. If your punch commences with the right hand too high, you will create tension in the arm, chest, and shoulder. As your weight shifts forward into the left foot, three things happen at once: your torso and hips rotate left, your right fist punches straight forward while turning palm-down, and your left hand turns palm-up while retracting to your waist. In early stages of learning, you should not attempt to generate any power; just make a snap rotation of your waist at the end of the movement while keeping your arm completely relaxed throughout. "Waist" really means *waist*—not hips. If your waist is properly relaxed, the hips will rotate forward fractionally sooner than the torso, causing a small stretching in the musculature connecting the torso and hips. This stretching effectively stores energy, which is released when the waist itself rotates forward. If the waist is stiff, the torso will simply move as a block along with the hips, and no energy will be stored (this is like doing Karate or western boxing). *The body cannot store energy unless it is relaxed*. Li Yi Yu expresses the matter more evocatively: "The shoulders follow the turning of the waist like a dragon twisting its body."

The foregoing description is, of course, highly simplified. The waist is not actually a single unit. It consists of numerous small articulations, each of which stores and releases energy in the manner described above. The feet, legs, arms, and hands act in like fashion, with every joint and process amplifying the power of its neighbors in the chain: as one releases, it stores power in the next, and each successive release contains the combined power of its predecessors. It is like cracking a whip, where each tiny segment of the whip is self-powered and contributes to the force issued at the tip. *Fa jin*, therefore, is a coordinated, explosive, plyometric chain-reaction.[6] Because it is plyometric, it also trains speed and flexibility.

It should be obvious that *fa jin* requires extraordinarily precise coordination—or, to state the matter in our own terms, *deep* coordination, conscious relaxation, and coherent movement. It can only be learned through years of correct Taiji practice.

Here are some further points to observe:

- Do not fixate on the attacking hand. Part of your awareness should stay centered on the *dan tian* and waist.

- The rotation of your torso should occur directly along the axis of your spine; off-axis movement dissipates your force. This is one reason why the spine always remains straight.

- Your head should neither tilt nor turn throughout the movement; it faces straight forward.

- Exhale through the nose as you punch, then abruptly close off the exhalation when your waist terminates its travel. The closing is instantaneous; your breathing should continue normally immediately afterward.

- Do not uproot yourself. In other words, do not jump up or forward off your back foot. *Fa jin* generates power from coherent movement, not from throwing one's weight around.

- The left elbow retracts with the same force as the right hand's extension. If your right hand feels uncoordinated in practice, concentrate on the left for a while. It is a common mistake to become preoccupied with the attacking hand.

- As always, no joint should ever extend to the point where it locks. Your right hand should stop before the elbow locks.

- Your back foot must not move at all. Even a slight movement of the back foot causes a diffusion of energy. You can demonstrate this to yourself by striking a heavy bag with the technique in this example. If you allow the back foot to move, you will find that a substantial amount of energy recoils back through your body and dissipates. If the back foot stays rooted, all of the energy goes into the target. Experienced practitioners can shake the room with their *fa jin* because of the energy driving into the rooted foot.

Taiji movements, including *fa jin*, are structurally balanced. This is because power is generated through rotation around an axis (namely, the waist and spine), even when the attack itself travels in a straight line (in our example, the right hand goes straight to the target). As a result, there is no point in the movement where you are physically committed; you can check your attack at any time without ending in a compromised position, even for an instant. This is the meaning of Wu Yu Xiang's advice, "Seek the straight in the curved."

The example presented here is a good one for learning because it employs a long motion with a weight shift, and the force issues at a right angle to the axis of rotation. Other examples of *fa jin* (including several in the First Form) use very short movements, no weight shift, and issue force in a variety of directions. These are harder for the beginner but are all exactly the same once the technique is learned. Deep coordination allows you to translate the energy in your joints in the same way that a high jumper translates forward momentum into lift.

Deep coordination and coherent movement are prerequisites for *fa jin*. This is not to say that you must master these skills before attempting to practice *fa;* it simply means that it is physically impossible to do *fa* correctly without first having acquired some ability in the other two.

Real *fa jin* is unmistakable and resembles no other physical performance. I once took a friend to watch a demonstration given by one of the top contemporary Chen Style masters. After the demonstration, my friend commented on the master's *fa jin*. "What was that about?" he said. "It looked like something went off inside of him."

The correct practice of *fa jin* is extremely subtle. In this section I've presented some guidelines based on a simplified breakdown. These guidelines do not by themselves comprise correct practice. If you follow them carefully, stay completely relaxed, and train daily, you will eventually find your own way. As with everything in Taiji, however, you should not expect quick results. My most talented students generally start showing some evidence of Taiji body mechanics after about a year and a half of training.

## ⠶ Chapter 5

# Forms

## 5.1 The Purpose of Forms

Chen Style Taiji is perhaps the most overtly martial of all Taiji styles. Most Chen Style forms are fast. These include Second Form (Cannon Bashing), saber, double saber, spear, long staff, short staff, three-opponent staff, glaive, punching bags, and several combat exercises. The only two forms that are decidedly slow are the First Form and the straight sword.[1]

Why, then, are some forms practiced rapidly and others slowly?

This question poses a fairly profound mystery even for some experienced Taijiquan practitioners. The answer, however, is quite simple.

Traditional teaching asserts that the purpose of forms is to train the waist. This is true, but the waist is only one part of the whole. Taiji forms (as the reader should now know) train body mechanics. Taiji's body mechanics encompass basic principles of alignment and posture, and also the more esoteric principles of deep coordination and coherent movement. Alignment and posture can, in some sense, be trained at any tempo, but deep coordination and coherent movement can only be trained slowly (at least in early stages); beginners invariably lose connection when trying to move fast.

Conversely, kinetic movements (meaning, again, movements that depend on momentum) must be trained at speed. Any time you have a weapon in your hands that swings or spins, you must actually swing it or spin it in order to learn its behavior. If you try to practice it slowly, you will not receive feedback from the weapon's own kinetic properties, and will consequently never learn how to exploit them. Without kinetic training, you will always be fighting the weapon.

In certain situations, you need to wield your own body kinetically. Chen Taiji's Second Form (Cannon Bashing) is designed for exactly that purpose. Any movement in which you sweep, leap, close quickly with the opponent, change orientation in mid-air, or swing around to attack from a different direction must similarly be trained at speed. These are all movements that exploit the body's mass and momentum.

Now—why is the straight sword a slow form?

The answer, quite predictably, is that the Chinese straight sword is not a kinetic weapon. It is a fairly light blade used mostly for thrusting. Later versions (including the type familiar to Taiji's inventors) were designed with a slightly heavier blade in order to enable use of the edge, but using the edge of the straight sword requires a completely different technique than using the edge of the saber. The straight sword will not cut if you swing it in a constant-radius arc; it will "hack" (that is, it will chop into the target and stop). The curved saber, by contrast, will cut smoothly unless it strikes the target at a right angle to the blade. In order to cut with a straight sword, you must draw it in an arc of diminishing radius. This is a very controlled, non-kinetic movement. There are some fast movements in the straight sword form, but, not surprisingly, they are all hacking movements. As a consequence of these and related considerations, the straight sword requires much more skill to wield than any other bladed weapon (it is also the most difficult exercise in Chen Style Taiji). This is why the Chinese military phased out its use in battle from the Eastern Han dynasty on; it is nearly impossible to train an entire army in such subtle techniques.

If you are familiar with the Old Chen Style, you will find that these principles of fast and slow training are *completely* consistent across every move of every form in the system. Kinetic movements are executed rapidly in slow forms and non-kinetic movements are executed slowly in fast forms; *fa jin* is always fast. There are no exceptions.

New forms, however, are a different matter. I frequently advise my students to suspect the utility of any form that was developed after the time that the weapon was in actual use (this, of course, applies to any martial art—not just Taiji). Completely slow saber forms, for example, are simply wrong. There are also various "competition forms" that were devised in recent decades for the purpose of standardizing the judging of martial-arts tournaments. These forms may have aesthetic or calisthenic value, but they are generally compromised as martial art. Many modern sword forms, for example, contain serious technical flaws such as twisting thrusts, thrusts with a blade orientation perpendicular to major bones in the target region, incorrect presentation of target aspect, and, of course, general confusion about kinetic and non-kinetic movement. All of these issues were implicit knowledge to foot soldiers of ancient times but are now unknown even to many masters. There is reason to be thankful for teachers who preserve what they were taught, even if they are unsure exactly why.

## 5.2 The Practice of Forms

Beginning students have a tendency to cling to the sanctity of details (which they can see) rather than the sanctity of principles (which they do not yet understand). It can therefore be confusing to see the same form executed differently by different people or by the same person at different times. These discrepancies have partly to do with individual variations in body type and physical capabilities, and partly to do with deliberate variations in execution.

When you first learn a Taiji form, proper coordination must be trained at a gross level before it can be refined. Your movements therefore begin large and become smaller over time, as your skill increases. Beginner forms (that is, beginners' versions of Taiji forms) contain large, clear postures, whereas experts' movements are sometimes so subtle that certain aspects disappear entirely from view. Waist movements, for example, may shrink in magnitude until they are nothing but a deep, internal rotation of the *dan tian*; transitional steps may be elided altogether. At the highest levels of mastery, forms may look almost casual or goofy because Taiji's deep coordination permits tremendous freedom. Beginner forms generally look better to inexperienced observers because the movements are more explicit.

As a consequence, some experts actually modify their forms for demonstration purposes by making the movements larger or by performing them at greater speed. The forms themselves contain some room for variation. They may be performed with high, medium, or low stances; certain individual movements have more than one legitimate version; some movements may optionally be executed with *fa*. And so on.

The point is that you should not be alarmed if you see your form demonstrated differently from how you learned it, even if the demonstrator is your own teacher. As a beginner, your job is to concentrate on proper fundamentals (as outlined in Chapter 4), and to practice without "breaking energy." This means two things:

- Your movements must be temporally continuous. From the beginning of your form to the end, you must never stop moving. You must do this while making every posture complete and distinct, and without allowing one posture to "blur" into the next. If your practice area is too small to contain the whole form, it is permissible to adjust your position within the available space by changing the size or direction of your steps, or by adding extra steps; however, you must do this without interrupting the form.

- Your movements must be coherent. You will not achieve truly coherent movement for many years, but you must have the intention of doing so from the very beginning. This means that your body must remain completely relaxed and your movements must be coordinated so that no part is "broken" from the whole.

When you practiced the standing exercise in Chapter 4, you learned the challenge of holding your entire posture in your mind at once. This is even more difficult when your body is moving. It requires a very agile awareness. Part of your awareness stays centered on the *dan tian*, part goes to the point of application, and part suffuses your entire body. You should pay particular attention that your mind does not fixate tensely on any one area while neglecting the rest. The locus of your attention may move, but its boundaries never narrow.

The beginner has no sense of her *dan tian,* so she must first surrender her preoccupation with hands and feet and learn to focus on the center of her body. This is not, however, the final objective. When facing an opponent, the center of your awareness follows your intention, but awareness itself must be everywhere at once.

When practicing the First Form, you should not try to control your breathing except when issuing (in which case you should breathe as described on page 81). Simply breathe naturally through your nose.

One iteration of the First Form can take from about eight to twenty minutes to complete. Beginners cannot do the form in less than about ten minutes without completely losing coordination. Slower practice is also more physically demanding than fast practice. Your legs will hurt for at least the first year or two of training; if they do not, then either your stances are too high or you are rushing. Your general pace (accounting for tempo variations in individual movements) should remain constant from beginning to end. Do not speed up when you start to feel the burn (good teachers abhor this particular failing because it shows poor discipline and even an ounce or two of self-deception). If you train properly, then this is the hardest physical work you will ever do.

My own teacher refuses to look at his students in the morning until they have completed ten iterations of the First Form—a two-and-a-half-hour ordeal that serves as a preliminary warm-up before any real work can begin. On some days his students will do fifteen to twenty repetitions in continuous sets of five or ten. This level of training is necessary for anyone aspiring to become a serious martial artist.

Many Western Taiji practitioners, however, have other aspirations. One daily iteration of the First Form will provide some benefit as exercise, though to make progress in Taiji it is certainly necessary to do at least two or three. The best way to practice multiple repetitions is to do them continuously. Connect them together so that the last repetition of Diamond King Pounds Mortar (see the next section) becomes the first one in the next repetition of the form. If you do not have available a single block of time in which to practice all of your repetitions, then they may be spread throughout the day.

## 5.3 Chen Style Old Frame, First Form

The form presented in this section is in the lineage of Chen Qing Zhou, nineteenth-generation successor and disciple of Chen Zhao Pei. Because Chen Qing Zhou is the only important nineteenth-generation lineage holder who never studied New Frame, his forms retain a high degree of fidelity—meaning that they are unaffected by New Frame's elaborate circles.

The illustrations that follow represent a "medium" performance. The stances are of approximately medium width and height, and the movements are mostly direct, though a few "large" transitions are retained for the sake of clarity. It is assumed that the reader has read and understood Chapter 4. Details of basic hand

and foot techniques (including issues such as weight shifting) are not repeated in the following narrative.

For reference purposes, we refer to the direction you are facing when you begin the form as "south." All other compass directions are relative to this.

## ✖ Movement #1:
## Opening Movement *(Taiji Chu Shi)*

1. Stand in Basic Posture with feet shoulder width apart and hands at your sides. Palms face medially (see figure 5.1).

2. From here until the end of the form, listening focuses behind you. Weight sinks slightly. As the *dan tian* moves back toward the spine, both hands turn palm-down and rise in front of the body until they are one or two inches lower than shoulder level. The arms maintain a slight, constant curvature throughout this movement (see figure 5.2).

*Figure 5.1*    *Figure 5.2*    *Figure 5.3*

3. As both hands move down and in toward the waist (with the palms still facing down), weight sinks into a horse stance with slightly more weight on the right leg. The *dan tian* and waist

relax. Hands end at waist level, slightly in front of the body
(see figure 5.3).

## ✖ Movement #2: **Diamond King Pounds Mortar** *(Jin Gang Dao Dui)*

The four Diamond Kings *(Jin Gang)* are guardian deities whose
images flank the entrances to Buddhist temples. The name of this
movement is usually translated (rather verbosely) as "Buddha's
Warrior Attendant Pounds Mortar."

1. Right palm turns to face left as both
   hands press forward and to the left
   at a forty-five-degree angle. Toward
   the end of their travel, both hands
   arc slightly upward. Weight simultaneously shifts to the left leg, but
   the left hip does not pass outside
   the left foot (see figure 5.4).

2. Right foot steps backward and
   right at a forty-five-degree angle.
   The toe of the right foot points
   southwest. Then, simultaneously:

*Figure 5.4*

- Weight shifts seventy percent to the right leg.

- Right toe turns to point west.

- Waist turns right until the axis through the shoulders points
  directly south.

- Hands rise to collarbone level while the left palm turns up
  and the right palm turns out (faces away from the body). The

hands maintain approximately the same relative distance to the body as where they ended in step (1), above, and also the same relative distance from each other (equal to the length of a forearm from wrist to elbow). They follow the turning of the waist so that they pull to the right as the waist turns.

Eyes continue to look south throughout this entire step (see figure 5.5).

3. Weight shifts entirely to the right leg. Left knee lifts while the left ankle remains flexed (do not point the toe). This causes the left foot to sweep up, ending close to the right knee. As the left foot comes up, both hands pull very slightly northward (see figure 5.6).

4. Weight sinks low on the right leg. Left foot slide-steps twenty-five degrees to the left (twenty-five degrees east of south). When the left foot stops, both hands circle up and back with the palms facing out as the waist turns slightly right. Eyes may briefly look back at the hands as they move (see figure 5.7).

*Figure 5.5*

*Figure 5.6*

*Figure 5.7*

5. Both hands continue circling back and down without pause. When they reach diaphragm level, simultaneously:

- Eyes look south.

- Weight shifts forward onto the left leg while the left toe turns to point south.

- Waist turns slightly left.

- Right hand continues down to waist level, then turns palm-up and trails behind the body.

- Left elbow moves straight forward (parallel to the plane of the body) at diaphragm level while the forearm remains horizontal and the palm faces down. The left forearm is close to the body (see figure 5.8).

Figure 5.8

6. Left toe turns out slightly as the waist turns left and the left hand (still palm-down) moves forward, away from the body. The right hand then swings down and forward with the palm facing forward. At the same time, the right foot steps forward into empty stance (weight remains on the left), and the left hand (palm side leading) arcs up and in toward the chest, meeting the right upper arm just as it reaches its forward position. The left palm ends facing right (see figure 5.9).

Figure 5.9

7. Without pausing, the left hand continues to circle downward (remaining close to the body), ending palm-down directly in front of the *dan tian*. At the same time, the right hand continues its arc forward, up, and in until it is directly in front of the nose (the palm does not turn, so it now faces in), where it makes a fist. Next, the left palm turns up as the right fist descends to meet it (the fifth-finger side of the fist makes contact with the left palm), and weight sinks deeper onto the left leg (see figure 5.10).

8. The right fist rises straight up in front of the nose with the forearm vertical. At the same time, the right knee rises (see figure 5.11).

9. The right fist drops sharply down into the left palm (again, the fifth-finger side of the fist makes contact) as weight sinks and the right foot drops sharply and flatly to the floor with a stamp (foot meets floor at the same time as fist meets palm). The right foot lands almost parallel to the left (as always, the toes point out slightly), and about shoulder-width apart. Weight remains on the *left* foot (see figure 5.12).

Figure 5.10

Figure 5.11

Figure 5.12

If practicing on a hard surface, be careful not to stamp with too much force (in this movement or any other). You should avoid stressing your joints.

## ✛ Movement #3: Lazily Tucking Clothes (*Lan Zha Yi*)

1. Right hand opens with the palm facing up. The right hand moves left as the left hand moves right until the fingertips of both hands are close to the opposite elbow (see figure 5.13).

2. The palms of both hands turn out (rotating medially), then the right hand arcs away from the body, past the face and to the right, as the left hand arcs down and to the left. When the hands begin to separate, weight shifts to the right foot. As the left hand passes the left foot, the left foot steps directly to the left (see figure 5.14).

3. Both hands continue the circles begun in the previous step: the right hand travels down, left, and up, while the left hand turns palm-up (rotating laterally) and travels up, right, and down. At the same time, weight shifts to the left leg. Then, simultaneously:

*Figure 5.13*

*Figure 5.14*

- Hands end crossed in front of the chest, with the left wrist or forearm resting on the right elbow. The right hand extends slightly away from the body as it crosses with the left. The right palm now faces up and the left palm faces right or down.

- Weight sinks onto the left leg, and the right foot slide-steps right.

- Eyes look to the right (see figure 5.15).

4. Right palm turns to face out (rotating medially). As weight shifts right into a side bow-stance, the right hand arcs up and right as the left hand moves to the left hip and rests there. When the right hand reaches the end of its travel, the right arm should align with the right thigh. Correct extension for the right arm is about two inches less than maximum extension. Next, the head turns to face center while the eyes continue to look at the tip of the right middle finger. At the same time, the *dan tian* relaxes, and the right elbow and weight sink just slightly (see figure 5.16).

*Figure 5.15*

*Figure 5.16*

## ✖ Movement #4: **Six Sealing, Four Closing (*Liu Feng Si Bi*)**

1. Left hand moves toward the right hand (see figure 5.17).

2. As weight sinks and shifts left, the waist turns slightly left and both hands pull back (to the left) and down, maintaining a forearm-length separation. After the left hand passes the left hip, it continues to travel left as the palm turns up (rotating laterally). When the right hand reaches the left hip, both hands begin to travel up: the right hand arcs toward the left shoulder while the left hand keeps pace to its left. When the right hand passes the left shoulder, it continues toward the left side of the neck while the palm rotates medially to face out. At the same time, the left hand continues its arc up to head level and in toward the left side of the neck, also rotating medially so that the palm faces out. As the palms rotate, the elbows push out slightly (so that the fingers tip in) and weight sinks again. Throughout this step, eyes may watch the hands, but at the end, eyes look right (see figure 5.18).

*Figure 5.17*

*Figure 5.18*

3. Right toe turns out and weight shifts to the right foot as the waist turns slightly right (the torso should face about twenty degrees west of south). Then, simultaneously:

- Left foot steps to the right, ending in a south-facing, right-weighted empty-stance, with the torso still facing about twenty degrees right.

- Both hands push forward at a forty-five-degree angle to the right while both elbows rotate down, but not all the way. Hands end at mid-chest level, the right slightly higher than the left, and elbows are moderately bent. The right elbow is slightly more extended than the left.

- Sink the *dan tian* and weight slightly onto the right leg as the hands complete their travel (see figure 5.19).

*Figure 5.19*

## ✕ Movement #5: **Single Whip *(Dan Bian)***

The name "Single Whip" in Chinese *(dan bian)* is a homophone for another expression meaning *"dan tian* change." Some sources claim that the latter is the original name for this movement; however, based on the fact that several Shaolin forms and Qi Ji Guang's "Boxing Classic" contain a clearly analogous posture called "Single Whip," I believe this name to be the original. It was probably changed somewhere down the line for didactic purposes.

1. Weight sinks slightly on the right leg (again). As weight sinks, the right hand drops slightly. Then, simultaneously:

- Waist turns slightly left so that the torso faces south.

- Left hand circles down so that it ends palm-up under the starting position of the right elbow. The left forearm is approximately horizontal and close to the body.

- Right hand circles down and left to a position just outside the left elbow. At the same time, the right elbow pushes outside the left hand. At this point, the two forearms are about parallel, with the left forearm lower and closer to the body than the right.

Next, the right hand becomes a downward-pointing hook hand (see figure 5.20).

2. Right hand extends up and right so that the wrist is level with the shoulder and the arm points about seventy degrees west of south. At the same time, the left hand withdraws so that it is against the body and directly below the *dan tian*. Look slightly left (see figure 5.21).

*Figure 5.20*

*Figure 5.21*

3. Left foot slide-steps left, then the left hand arcs up near the right shoulder and turns palm-out (rotating medially). As weight

shifts left into a left-weighted bow stance, left hand continues its travel out (away from the body) and left, ending with the arm aligned with the left thigh and extended about two inches short of its maximum extension. The wrist is level with the shoulder, and eyes look at the tip of the middle left finger while the head faces front. Next, sink the *dan tian,* elbows, and weight (see figure 5.22).

Figure 5.22

## ✠ Movement #6: **Diamond King Pounds Mortar (Jin Gang Dao Dui)**

1. Right hand becomes an open palm as it arcs down and left, ending near the left hand. At the same time, eyes look left (see figure 5.23).

2. Maintaining a forearm-length separation, both hands pull up and back (right) as the left hand rotates (laterally) palm-up and the right hand rotates (medially) palm-out. At the same time, weight simultaneously sinks and shifts into a right-weighted squat-stance. The left toe is free to come up as this happens (see figure 5.24).

3. Both hands continue their arc back (right) and down, the right hand going to nearly full extension and the left hand going to

Figure 5.23         Figure 5.24         Figure 5.25

the right side of the torso. Next, without pausing, rise up and forward (left) into a left-weighted, front bow-stance as the left elbow comes forward (see figure 5.25).

4. Repeat steps (6)–(9) of Movement #2, this time facing east.

## ✕ Movement #7: **White Goose Spreads Wings** *(Bai E Liang Chi)*

"White goose spreads wings" *(bai e liang chi)* is a near-homophone for "white crane spreads wings" *(bai he liang chi)*. Chen villagers assert that Yang Lu Chan's illiteracy caused him to mistake the name when he taught Taijiquan to outsiders, leading to popularization of the latter version.

1. Repeat step (1) of Movement #3.

2. Both hands rotate medially so that the palms face out. Left hand arcs down and left as right hand arcs up, out, and right (apex of the arc is about head level). At the same time, weight shifts to the right leg. When the left hand passes the left thigh, the left foot steps backward at a forty-five-degree angle (see figure 5.26).

Figure 5.26　　　　　　　　Figure 5.27　　　　　　　　Figure 5.28

3. Both hands continue their circles as weight shifts back to the left leg. Left hand rotates laterally to a palm-up position and continues its arc up, forward, and down, while the right hand continues down, in, and up. Hands end crossed in front of the chest, left hand palm-down and right hand palm-up (see figure 5.27).

4. Right foot steps back at about a forty-five-degree angle relative to the left. The right palm turns out (rotating medially). As weight shifts back to the right foot, the hands separate: right hand arcs up and to the right, ending at head level, while the left hand arcs down and left, ending just above and outside the left knee. Both hands reach their terminus just as weight is fully on the right foot. At this point, the left foot retracts into empty stance (see figure 5.28).

## ✖ Movement #8: **Oblique Posture (Xie Xing)**

1. Waist turns left and both hands follow (see figure 5.29).

2. Right hand arcs down while the left hand turns palm-up (rotating laterally), extends, and arcs up. At the same time, the waist turns right and weight sinks (both hands follow the waist move-

ment). The right toe may turn out as this happens. As the waist reaches its maximum turn, the left foot slide-steps forward at a forty-five-degree angle (northeast), and the left hand extends a bit farther up (see figure 5.30).

3. Simultaneously:

- Weight shifts forward.

- Waist begins to turn left as the torso bends at the *kua* toward the left knee.

- Left hand descends in and down past the face, then the elbow leads in an arc down and around the left knee. The ideal trajectory for the elbow has it pass seven inches above the ground as it rounds the knee. Eyes watch the left hand after it passes the face.

- Right hand rises straight up from behind (rotating laterally to a palm-up orientation) and begins to arc in toward the head.

Throughout this entire movement, it is essential that the back remain perfectly straight, even while the *kua* flexes to bring the elbow down (see figure 5.31).

Figure 5.29                    Figure 5.30                    Figure 5.31

4. The left elbow continues its arc past the left knee while the right hand continues toward the back of the head. Eyes are still watching the left hand. As the left hand passes the knee, it becomes a downward-pointing hook hand. Then, simultaneously:

   - The torso rises into a vertical position as the waist continues to turn left.
   - The left wrist leads in an upward arc to a position about forty-five degrees forward and left of the left shoulder. The left arm straightens some as this happens, but remains slightly curved.
   - The right hand passes the right side of the head and continues past the face to push toward the inside of the left elbow. Eyes watch the right hand as it passes the face (see figure 5.32).

5. Waist turns slightly right and weight shifts slightly back as the right hand opens outward in a shoulder-level arc to the right. Eyes are still looking at the right hand. The left hand remains in place, so the left arm extends slightly as the torso moves away from it (see figure 5.33).

Figure 5.32

Figure 5.33

*Figure 5.34a*

*Figure 5.34b*

6. Waist turns left (ends facing east) and both arms follow (maintaining their positions relative to the torso; the arms are extended out from the shoulders and slightly forward, and the chest is concave). At the same time, *dan tian*, elbows, and weight sink. Look forward (see figures 5.34a and 5.34b).

## ✖ Movement #9: **Embrace Knee (Lou Xi)**

1. Weight sinks and shifts back to the right leg as the hips turn slightly right. At the same time, left hand becomes open palm as both hands "scoop" down to about knee level and up to about diaphragm level with the palm side leading. The right hand draws in closer to the body as it scoops, leaving the left hand farther in front (see figure 5.35).

2. Left foot retracts into empty stance as both hands continue their upward travel, the left hand rising to about collarbone level and the right hand rising to about mid-chest level. The two hands line up on an east-west axis. Next, sink both wrists as

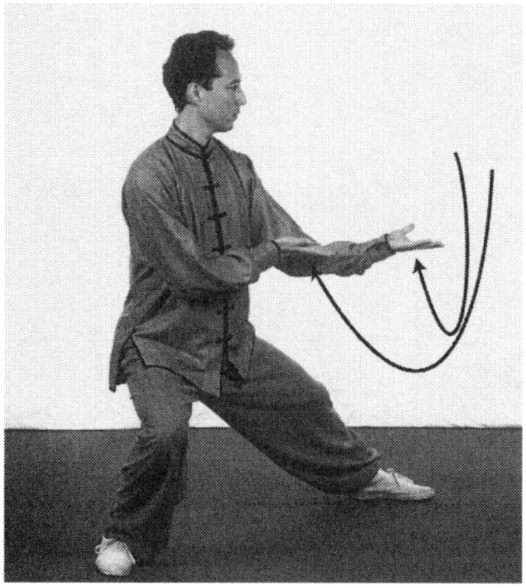

Figure 5.35

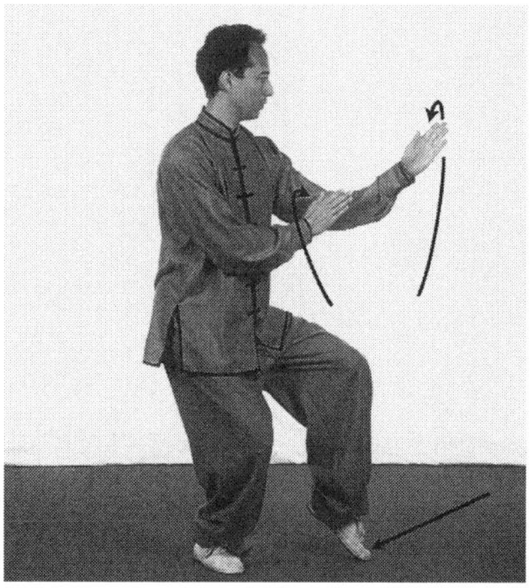

Figure 5.36

the hands rotate medially so that the right palm faces left and the left palm faces right. The fingertips point up at about a forty-five-degree angle and forward. At the same time, sink the *dan tian* and weight (see figure 5.36).

## Movement #10: **Twist Steps *(Ao Bu)***

1. Both hands arc down and back on the right side of the body. The left hand passes the right hip and continues up to the right shoulder, where it rotates medially so that the palm faces out. At the same time, the right hand continues to arc back. As the left hand passes the right side of the face, the left foot steps forward at a twenty- or thirty-degree angle (twenty or thirty degrees north of east) with the toes pointing straight east. Weight shifts to the left leg as the left hand extends straight forward, and the right hand continues to arc back and up (see figure 5.37).
2. The left hand continues its travel down to the left knee as the right hand turns palm-up (rotating laterally) and arcs to the

*Figure 5.37*

*Figure 5.38*

right side of the neck. As the left hand passes the knee, the waist turns slightly left (bringing the right elbow forward), and the left foot twists on the heel so that the toe points out. At the same time, weight shifts completely to the left leg. Next, the right foot steps forward at a twenty- or thirty-degree angle (twenty or thirty degrees south of east) with the toe pointing straight east. As weight shifts forward onto the right leg, the right hand extends straight forward and the left hand continues its arc back (see figure 5.38).

## ✖ Movement #11: **Oblique Posture (Xie Xing)**

1. Right hand continues its arc down toward the right knee as the left hand arcs up and forward, maintaining its extension. At the same time, the waist turns right (the left hand following in a high, rightward arc), the right toe turns out, and all weight shifts to the right leg. As the waist approaches its maximum

rightward turn, the
left foot slide-steps
forward at a forty-
five-degree angle
(northeast), and the
left hand extends a
bit farther out and
up (see figure 5.39).

2. Repeat steps (3)–(6)
of Movement #8.

*Figure 5.39*

## ✖ Movement #12: **Embrace Knee (Lou Xi)**

Repeat Movement #9.

## ✖ Movement #13: **Twist Steps (Ao Bu)**

Repeat Movement #10.

## ✖ Movement #14: **Covered Hand Punch (Yan Shou Hong Quan)**

1. Weight shifts completely to the right leg as the right toe turns
   out and the waist turns right. At the same time, the left hand
   turns palm-up (rotating laterally) and begins to arc upward as
   the right hand retracts slightly and sinks lower. Next, the left
   foot steps forward and forty-five degrees to the left. At the same
   time, the left hand arcs forward and down to cover the right
   (hands cross just when the left foot lands). Hands end crossed

at the wrist with both palms facing down (see figure 5.40).

2. Left hand arcs down and forward as the right hand arcs down and back. At the same time, weight shifts forward onto the left leg (at this point, the toe of the right foot may turn a bit toward the front). Then, simultaneously:

Figure 5.40

- Left hand continues its arc upward, rising to mid-chest level. The arm is extended straight forward and the palm faces down.

- Right hand rotates laterally into a palm-up position while becoming a fist and circling up to rest at the bottom of the right side of the rib cage.

- Weight shifts back to the right leg as the waist turns a bit farther to the right.

*Dan tian* and weight sink (see figure 5.41).

Figure 5.41

3. Simultaneously:

- Weight shifts smoothly forward onto the left leg as the waist rotates left.

- Left hand turns palm-up (rotating laterally) and withdraws to the left side of the rib cage.

Figure 5.42

• Right hand punches straight forward at chest level while the fist turns palm-down (rotating medially). The back of the right hand should end level with the forearm.

This movement is executed with *fa jin* (see figure 5.42).

## ✂ Movement #15: **Diamond King Pounds Mortar** (*Jin Gang Dao Dui*)

1. Left hand arcs up (palm side leading) to the inside of the right elbow as the right hand becomes an open palm. Left hand pushes straight down while the right hand arcs up (rotating medially to a palm-out orientation) and right at head level. At the same time, weight shifts back to the right leg while waist, hips, and right foot turn right. When weight has shifted to the right leg, the left toe turns in. End facing south in a right-weighted, front bow-stance (see figure 5.43).

2. As weight shifts to the left leg, the left hand arcs up (rotating palm-up laterally) to about shoulder level, while the right hand begins to arc back and down (also to shoulder level). Then, simultaneously:

   • The toe of the right foot slides on the ground, moving in a "U" shape synchronously with the right hand as it contin-

*Figure 5.43*

*Figure 5.44*

ues its arc back and down (toward the north, but not behind the plane of the torso), down and in toward the right hip, then forward. The arm maintains its extension throughout this movement, and the palm side of the hand leads. End in a left-weighted empty-stance.

- Left hand continues its arc up and forward (south), then in toward the right side of the chest (palm side leads). It meets the right upper arm just as the right arm and right foot are coming forward (see figure 5.44).

3. Repeat steps (7)–(9) of Movement #2.

## ✖ Movement #16: **Angled Body Fist (Pie Shen Quan)**

1. Left foot takes a small step to the left as the right fist becomes an open palm (palm faces up, fingers point left). Weight sinks into a horse stance as the hands separate, left hand moving left and right hand moving right. The hands remain palm-up as

*Figure 5.45*                     *Figure 5.46*

they separate, with the wrists leading the movement. When the arms are at about a forty-five-degree angle from the shoulder, both hands rotate laterally to a palm-up position as they continue their travel up and slightly forward to head level, then in toward the center and down. They end crossed at the wrists, directly in front of the chest (right hand on the inside). *Dan tian* and weight sink again as the hands cross (see figure 5.45).

2. The waist turns forty-five degrees left, and both hands extend sharply to the southeast and up at a forty-five-degree angle (eyes follow hands). At the same time, the right foot slide-steps right (west). The hands and the right foot stop at the same time (see figure 5.46).

3. Simultaneously:

   • Weight shifts to the right leg as the waist turns right and the torso bends deeply at the *kua* toward the right knee. The back remains perfectly straight.

   • The right elbow bends and travels in an arc toward the right knee, then below and around it.

- The left hand trails behind the movement of the torso, then begins to travel toward the left side of the head as the right elbow rounds the knee (see figure 5.47).

4. The right elbow continues its arc past the right knee while the left hand continues toward the back of the head. Eyes watch the right hand. As the right hand passes the knee, it becomes a downward-pointing hook hand. Then, simultaneously:

*Figure 5.47*

- The torso rises into a vertical position as the waist continues to turn right.

- The right wrist leads in an upward arc to a position about forty-five degrees forward and right of the right shoulder. The right arm straightens some as this happens but remains slightly curved.

- The left hand passes the left side of the head and continues past the face to push toward the inside of the right elbow. Eyes follow the left hand as it passes the face (see figure 5.48).

5. Waist turns slightly left (ends facing west) as the left hand travels

*Figure 5.48*

Figure 5.49a

Figure 5.49b

outward in a shoulder-level arc to the left (palm-out with wrist leading), ending in a position symmetrical with the right hand. Eyes still watch the left hand. The right hand remains in place, so the right arm extends slightly as the torso turns away from it. Next, the left wrist sinks so that the fingers point up while the *dan tian* and weight also sink (see figures 5.49a and 5.49b).

Figure 5.50

6. Waist turns slightly right. At the same time, the right hand becomes an open palm and arcs down to the right side (palm side leading) as the left hand moves slightly up (see figure 5.50).

7. Simultaneously:

   • Weight shifts to the left leg while the waist turns all the way left (torso ends facing east).

   • Right hand arcs up to shoulder level and around to the left, maintaining its extension and following the movement of the torso. The palm side leads the movement, and the hand ends with the fingers pointing directly east.

- Left hand rotates medially to a palm-down orientation as it arcs down to hip level and around to the left hip, following the movement of the torso (see figure 5.51).

*Figure 5.51*

8. Left hand rests on the top of the left hip as the right hand makes a fist. Weight shifts to the right leg, the left toe turns in, the right toe turns out, and the waist turns right as the right fist pulls back in a slight upward arc toward the right temple, simultaneously rotating medially until the palm side faces out. Eyes watch the left elbow. At the end of this movement, the left elbow and left toe should be in the same line of sight

*Figure 5.52*

(to achieve this, the torso cannot be aligned with the axis of the feet; it is twisted a bit farther to the right, and may tilt slightly forward at the *kua*). The right fist is one palm-width from the temple and legs are in a right-weighted, side bow-stance. Sink the *dan tian* and weight (see figure 5.52).

## ✖ Movement #17: **Green Dragon Emerges from Water** *(Qing Long Chu Shui)*

There are at least three distinct, equally valid versions of this movement. The version presented here was taught by Chen Zhao Pei late in his career; it is not commonly seen.

1. Simultaneously:

   - Weight shifts left as the waist turns a bit farther right and eyes look right.

   - Right forearm descends until it is about mid-chest level, then the elbow drops and the forearm gathers inward so that the forearm is vertical and directly in front of the right side of the chest.

   - Left hand (palm facing down) travels straight up over the top of the right forearm as the latter is descending, then down, and ends near the right elbow (see figure 5.53).

2. Waist rotates left as the right forearm snaps straight up (right fist ends at about nose level or slightly higher). At the same

*Figure 5.53*

*Figure 5.54*

time, the left hand retracts to the diaphragm while rotating (laterally) to a palm-up orientation. The right forearm and left elbow both travel with equal force, and the movement is executed with *fa jin* (see figure 5.54).

## ✠ Movement #18: **Two-Handed Push (Shuang Tui Shou)**

1. Weight shifts to the right leg as both hands turn palm-out and reach about sixty degrees to the right. The right hand leads the left by a forearm's length and ends its outward travel nearly fully extended at about head level (see figure 5.55).

2. Both hands pull down to hip level and around to the left side of the hip (left hand leading) as weight shifts to the left leg and the waist turns left (see figure 5.56).

3. As the torso continues to turn left with the hands following, the left toe turns out. While the hands continue their travel back and up (still maintaining their separation, and with the left

Figure 5.55

Figure 5.56

hand rotating laterally to a palm-up orientation), the right foot steps forty-five degrees to the right (southeast). The left hand continues its arc up to head level while the right hand continues to the left shoulder. Both hands then rotate medially to a palm-out orientation as they go to the left side of the neck. Both elbows point out slightly. Eyes look forty-five degrees right (see figure 5.57).

4. Weight shifts to the right foot and the torso turns toward the southeast. At the same time, both hands push forward (southeast) as the elbows rotate down (but not all the way). When weight is fully transferred to the right foot, the left foot steps forward and right (ending northeast of the right foot) into a right-weighted empty-stance. Hands end at mid-chest level (both hands at the same level, as distinct from Movement #4) with the elbows slightly bent. *Dan tian* and weight sink (see figure 5.58).

*Figure 5.57*

*Figure 5.58*

# ✠ Movement #19: **Fist Under Elbow (Zhou Xia Kan Quan)**

The "fist," in Old Chen Style's version of this movement, is actually an open palm. New Chen Style uses an actual fist, perhaps in an effort to make the movement correspond more closely to the name.

1. As the weight sinks low (and the back remains perfectly straight), the right hand arcs up and the left hand arcs down to the left. The right hand reaches its apex almost fully extended above and slightly forward of the right shoulder, while the left hand reaches its nadir almost fully extended down the left side (see figure 5.59).

2. Left hand continues its arc up to the left (rotating laterally to a palm-up orientation) as the right hand continues its arc down to the right. At the same time, weight rises a bit. When the left hand reaches its apex (almost fully extended above and slightly forward of the left shoulder) and the right hand reaches its nadir (almost fully extended down the right side), the left elbow sinks

Figure 5.59

Figure 5.60

straight down to a position in front of the lower left side of the chest. At the same time, the right hand rises to meet it, ending palm-up just underneath the elbow, and the weight and *dan tian* again sink (see figure 5.60).

## ✖ Movement #20: **Step Back and Swing Arms (*Dao Nian Hong*)**

This movement is often called *dao juan hong,* which translates roughly the same way in English.

1. Left hand turns palm-out (rotating medially) as the right hand turns palm-down (also rotating medially). Left hand pushes straight forward from the shoulder (ending nearly extended) as the right hand arcs down to the right side and back. As the left hand continues down to the left knee, the right hand turns palm-up (rotating laterally) and continues up to the right side of the neck (see figure 5.61).

Figure 5.61

2. As the left hand continues down and back past the left knee, the left foot steps back at about a twenty-five-degree angle (twenty-five degrees north of west). Then, simultaneously:

• Weight shifts back to the left leg as the waist turns slightly left. As soon as the weight begins to shift, the right toe turns straight forward (east).

- Right hand pushes straight forward from the shoulder, reaching nearly full extension as about seventy percent of the weight is on the left leg.

- Left hand continues its travel back and up, revolving from the shoulder (see figure 5.62).

3. Left hand turns palm-up (rotating laterally) as it continues up to the left side of the neck. At the same time, the right hand arcs down to the right knee. As the right hand passes the knee, the right foot steps back at about a twenty-five-degree angle (twenty-five degrees south of west). Then, simultaneously:

*Figure 5.62*

- Weight shifts back to the right leg as the waist turns slightly right. As soon as the weight begins to shift, the left toe turns straight forward (east).

- Left hand pushes straight forward from the shoulder, reaching nearly full extension as about seventy percent of the weight is on the right leg.

*Figure 5.63*

- Right hand continues its travel back and up, revolving from the shoulder (see figure 5.63).

4. Right hand turns palm-up (rotating laterally) as it continues up to the right side of the neck. At the same time, the left hand arcs down to the left knee. As the left hand passes the knee, the left foot steps back at about a twenty-five-degree angle (twenty-five degrees north of west). Then, simultaneously:

Figure 5.64

- Weight shifts back to the left leg as the waist turns slightly right. As soon as the weight begins to shift, the right toe turns straight forward (east).

- Right hand pushes straight forward from the shoulder, reaching nearly full extension as about seventy percent of the weight is on the left leg.

- Left hand continues its travel back and up, revolving from the shoulder (see figure 5.64).

5. Repeat step (3) of this movement.

## ✖ Movement #21: **White Goose Spreads Wings (Bai E Liang Chi)**

1. Left hand remains extended forward as the left foot steps back at a twenty-five-degree angle. At the same time, the right hand (also maintaining its extension) arcs up to about head level, forward, then down in front of the chest to about the same level as the left hand. Throughout this movement, the right arm revolves from the shoulder and the palm leads (see figure 5.65).

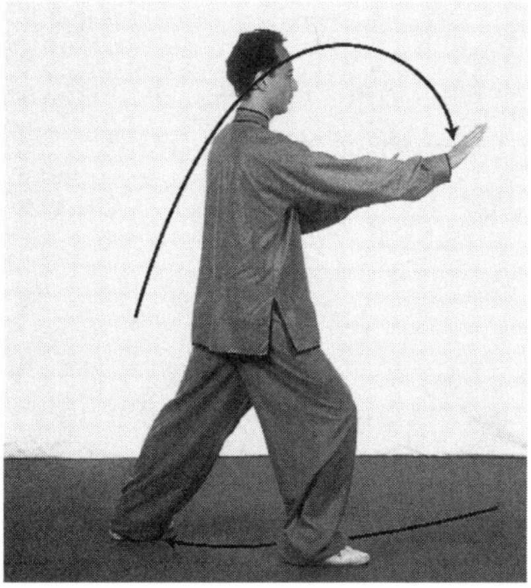

Figure 5.65

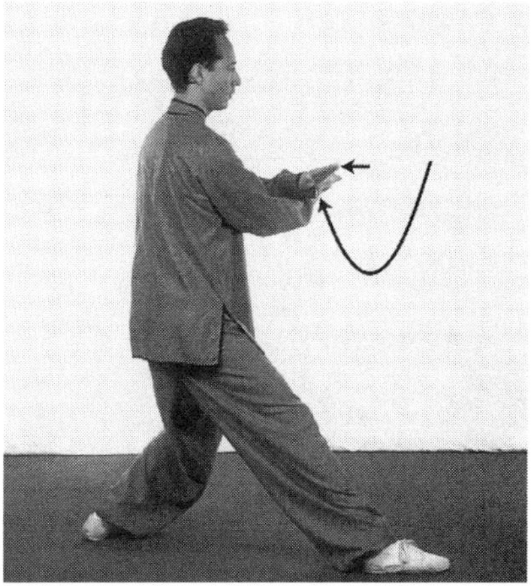

Figure 5.66

2. Weight shifts back to the left foot as the right hand continues its arc down past the left hand then turns up to cross underneath it. The arms end in front of the chest, crossed at the forearm. The right palm faces up and the left palm faces down (see figure 5.66).
3. Repeat Movement #7, step (4).

## Movement #22: **Oblique Posture** ***(Xie Xing)***

Repeat Movement #8.

## Movement #23: **Flash the Back** ***(Shan Tong Bei)***

1. The torso and hips turn slightly right, and weight shifts completely back to the right foot as both hands (palms leading) arc toward the center, then down to the right. The left hand is slightly forward (east) of the right hand throughout this movement.

Hands should reach the right side of the hip at the same time that the weight completes its shift to the right foot. At this point, the left foot steps back into a right-weighted empty-stance as the hands continue their travel: the left hand arcs up toward the right shoulder, and the right hand continues straight back (see figure 5.67).

2. Left hand turns palm-out (rotating medially) while the right hand turns palm-right (rotating laterally). The waist turns left (the torso ends facing east) as both hands sweep left, maintaining the same height and ending with palms facing left. The left hand stops forward of the left shoulder and about forty-five degrees to the left. The arm is bent. The right hand stops just above the inside of the left knee (see figure 5.68).

3. Simultaneously:

   • Weight sinks low and the waist turns right.

   • Left hand travels down and behind the back, where it becomes an upward-pointing hook hand. It ends resting at the base of the spine.

Figure 5.67

Figure 5.68

*Figure 5.69a*

*Figure 5.69b*

- Right hand turns palm-up as it travels up and over to the right side of the rib cage, where it rests with the fingers pointing slightly up.

Next, the left foot slide-steps forward at a thirty-degree angle (see figures 5.69a and 5.69b).

4. Weight shifts forward into a front bow-stance as the waist rotates left (to end facing east) and the right hand thrusts with force forward and up at a forty-five-degree angle, ending at head level. This movement is executed with *fa jin* (see figure 5.70).

5. Simultaneously:

- Weight shifts completely to the left leg as the entire body and both feet quickly turn nearly 180 degrees right.

*Figure 5.70*

*Figure 5.71*

*Figure 5.72*

- Right foot withdraws slightly closer to the body.

- Right hand follows the body's turn and begins to arc forward (west).

- Left hand unwinds from its position at the back and hangs ready at the left side (see figure 5.71).

6. The right hand chops straight down to the right side as the left hand swings up high. At the same time, the right knee rises up sharply. This movement is executed with *fa jin* (see figure 5.72).

## ✜ Movement #24: **Covered Hand Punch (Yan Shou Hong Quan)**

1. Jump straight up off the left foot and land with a stomp on the right. Weight immediately sinks, and the left foot steps forward at a forty-five-degree angle. At the same time, the hands come together to cross at the wrists, palm-down at diaphragm level with the left hand on top (see figure 5.73).

2. Repeat Movement #14, steps (2) and (3) (this time facing west).

## ✖ Movement #25: **Six Sealing, Four Closing (*Liu Feng Si Bi*)**

1. Right hand opens into a palm as the left hand arcs forward toward it (rotating palm-down). When the left hand is within a forearm's length of the right, both hands pull back and down toward the left hip as the waist turns left, the left foot turns out, and weight shifts completely to the left leg. As the hands continue past the left hip, the right foot steps straight forward (west of the left; see figure 5.74).

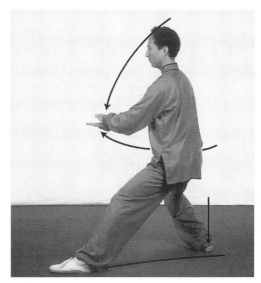

*Figure 5.73*

2. Both hands continue left. After the left hand passes the left hip, the palm turns up (rotating laterally). When the right hand reaches the left hip, both hands begin to travel up: the right hand arcs toward the

*Figure 5.74*

left shoulder while the left hand keeps pace to its left. When the right hand passes the left shoulder, it continues toward the left side of the neck while the palm rotates medially to face out. At the same time, the left hand continues its arc up to head level

*Figure 5.75*

and in toward the left side of the neck, also rotating medially so that the palm faces out. As the palms rotate, the elbows push out slightly (so that the fingers tip in) and weight sinks. Throughout this step, eyes may follow the hands, but at the end, eyes look right (see figure 5.75).

3. Repeat Movement #4, step (3).

## ✖ Movement #26: **Single Whip *(Dan Bian)***

Repeat Movement #5.

## ✖ Movement #27: **Hand Technique *(Yun Shou)***

The Chinese *yun shou* ("wield hands") is a homophone for another expression meaning "cloud hands." Yang Lu Chan's illiteracy may again have been responsible for popularization of the latter version.

The following narrative contains two repetitions of the movement, though the form is often practiced with three.

1. Right hand becomes open palm (facing down) and descends in an arc to a point below the navel. As the hand descends, it turns palm-in (rotating laterally) and crosses in front of the body so that the thumb is level with the navel. Eyes watch the left hand (see figure 5.76).

2. Simultaneously:

- Weight shifts right.

- Right hand continues past the navel and toward the left shoulder (rotating medially to a palm-out orientation), then out past the face at nose level and to the right. Eyes watch the right hand as it passes the nose, but the head faces south.

- Left hand descends in an arc to a point below the navel. As the hand descends, it turns palm-in (rotating laterally) and crosses in front of the body so that the thumb is level with the navel (see figure 5.77).

*Figure 5.76*

*Figure 5.77*

3. Simultaneously:

- Weight shifts left.

- Left hand continues past the navel and toward the right shoulder (rotating medially to a palm-out orientation), then out past the face at nose level and to the left. Eyes watch the left hand as it passes the nose, but the head does not move.

- Right hand descends in an arc to a point below the navel.

As the hand descends, it turns palm-in (rotating laterally) and crosses in front of the body so that the thumb is level with the navel.

When the right hand crosses the navel, the right foot steps in so that it is immediately adjacent and parallel to the left (see figure 5.78).

4. Simultaneously:

   - Weight shifts right.

   - Right hand continues past the navel and toward the left shoulder (rotating medially to a palm-out orientation), then out past the face at nose level and to the right. Eyes watch the right hand as it passes the nose, but the head does not move.

   - Left hand descends in an arc to a point below the navel. As the hand descends, it turns palm-in (rotating laterally) and crosses in front of the body so that the thumb is level with the navel. As the left hand crosses the navel, the left foot steps straight left, remaining parallel to the right (see figure 5.79).

5. Repeat steps (3) and (4) of this movement.

Figure 5.78                    Figure 5.79

# ✠ Movement #28: **High Pat on Horse** *(Gao Tan Ma)*

1. Torso, hips, and left foot turn ninety degrees left (east) as weight shifts to the left leg. The left hand rises slightly and follows the turning of the body. Next, the right foot steps forward (east) into a left-weighted empty-stance as the right hand arcs down and forward, ending crossed at the forearm under the left (see figure 5.80).

2. Right foot steps immediately back at a slight angle (about fifteen degrees south of west). As weight shifts back to the right foot, left hand turns palm out (rotating medially) and pushes straight forward (east). At the same, right hand arcs down and back past the right thigh (without rotating) and the waist turns slightly right. When the left hand reaches nearly full extension, it turns palm-up while the right hand rotates laterally and continues its arc up and in toward the right side of the neck. At the same time, weight sinks and the left toe turns in slightly (see figure 5.81).

*Figure 5.80* *Figure 5.81*

3. Simultaneously:

   - Body turns left (ends facing north) as the left foot slides on its toe straight west, past the right foot, and ends in a right-weighted empty-stance. Eyes continue to look east.

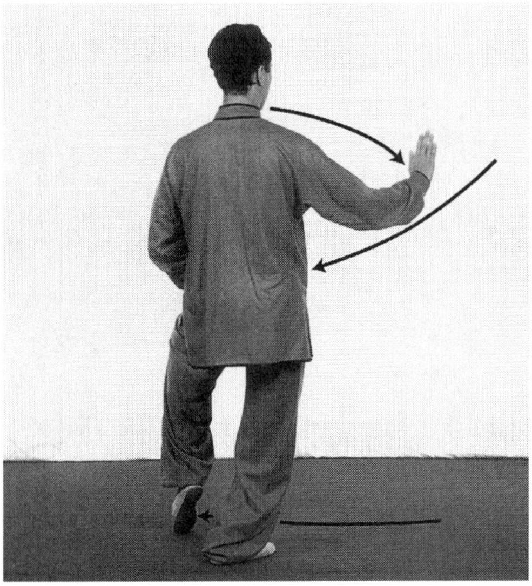

Figure 5.82

   - Right hand pushes right and down (to the right and slightly forward of the torso) with the outside edge of the hand leading as the elbow rotates down. The hand ends at mid-chest level with the arm slightly bent.
   - Left hand remains palm-up and withdraws to a position directly below the *dan tian* (see figure 5.82; figure 5.155b shows the correct position of the left hand, though the position of the right hand is slightly different).

## ⌘ Movement #29: Slap Right Foot *(You Ca Jiao)*

1. Left hand begins to rotate medially as it arcs toward the right hand (see figures 5.83a and 5.83b).
2. When the left hand is within a forearm's length of the right, both hands turn palm-down and pull down to the left while the weight sinks. The left hand makes a complete circle to the left side of the body, up to head level (rotating palm-up laterally), then to the right and down, while the right hand makes a

*Figure 5.83a*                    *Figure 5.83b*

half-circle, ending palm-up at the left side of the chest. As the left hand begins the upward part of its arc, the left foot rises and cross-steps to the right (synchronously with the motion of the left hand). Hands end crossed at the forearm at mid-chest level (see figures 5.84a and 5.84b).

*Figure 5.84a*                    *Figure 5.84b*

3. Weight sinks into a resting stance as the hands rotate medially to turn palm-out (see figures 5.85a and 5.85b).

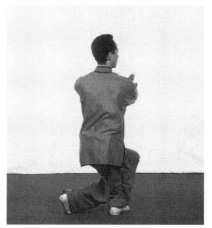

Figure 5.85a

Figure 5.85b

4. Weight rises on the left leg as the hands (remaining crossed) rise up above the head. As the right foot kicks up high to the right, both hands swing out and down. The right hand slaps the top of the right foot (making a sharp, distinct sound) at the top of the foot's arc (see figure 5.86).

Figure 5.86

## ✖ Movement #30: **Slap Left Foot (Zuo Ca Jiao)**

1. Simultaneously:

   • Right foot returns to the ground about shoulder's width east of the left foot, touching lightly on the heel, and immediately turns out to the right.

- Hips and torso turn about 150 degrees right as eyes continue to look east.

- Left hand arcs down and across to the right side of the chest while the right hand arcs down and up to the left side of the chest. The two hands meet at mid-chest level, crossed at the forearm, with the right palm up and the left palm down (see figure 5.87).

2. Hips and torso rotate further right (so that the axis through the shoulders runs east-west) as weight sinks into a resting stance and hands rotate medially to a palm-out orientation (see figure 5.88).

3. Weight rises on the right leg as the hands (remaining crossed) rise up above the head. As the left foot kicks up high to the left, both hands swing out and down. The left hand slaps the top of the left foot (making a sharp, distinct sound) at the top of the foot's arc (see figure 5.89).

Figure 5.87          Figure 5.88          Figure 5.89

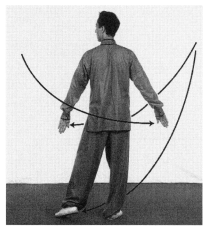

*Figure 5.90*

## ✕ Movement #31: **Left Heel Kick (Zuo Deng Yi Gen)**

1. The entire body and right foot quickly turn 180 degrees left as the left foot swings down behind the right leg and both hands lower from the shoulders so that the arms extend down and out from the body at about a thirty-degree angle. Look left (see figure 5.90).

2. Open palms become fists as both hands come together in front of the navel with palms facing in. At the same time, the left foot rises as far as possible up and in toward the left hip into a "cocked" position with the ankle flexed (see figures 5.91a and 5.91b).

*Figure 5.91a*

*Figure 5.91b*

3. Left heel kicks straight left with force as both fists rise up and swing straight out at shoulder level. Left foot and right hand issue *fa jin* with equal force (see figure 5.92).

Figure 5.92

## ✖ Movement #32: Advance Carefully with Twist Steps (*Qian Tang Ao Bu*)

1. Both hands become open palm. Left hand relaxes then makes a small vertical circle outward (west), with the edge of the hand leading. At the same time, the body and hips turn left and the left foot relaxes and steps west at about a twenty-five-degree angle (see figure 5.93).

2. Left hand arcs down toward the left knee, and the right hand travels to the right side of the neck (the palms of both hands lead the movement) as weight shifts forward onto the left leg. As the left hand passes outside the left knee,

Figure 5.93

the left foot turns out about forty-five degrees, body and hips turn left (bringing the right elbow forward), and the right foot steps forward at about a twenty-five-degree angle. The right

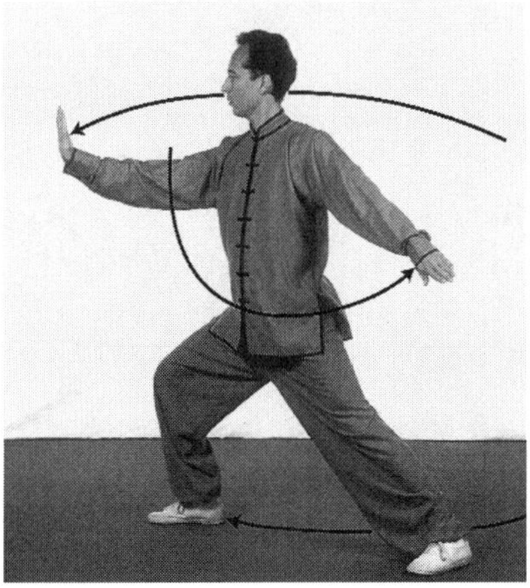

*Figure 5.94*

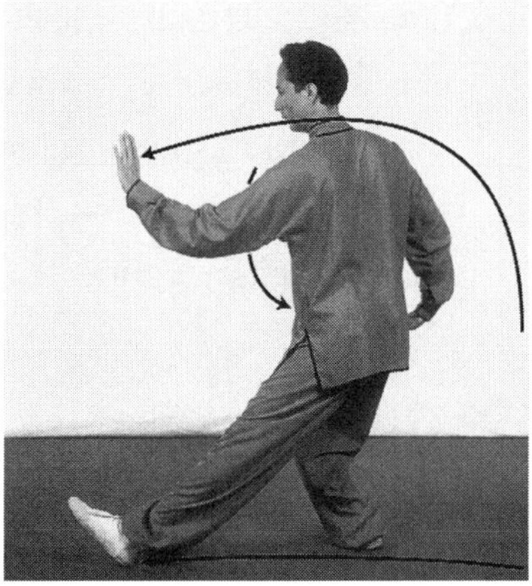

*Figure 5.95*

hand pushes straight forward from the shoulder as the left hand continues its arc back and weight shifts forward onto the right leg (see figure 5.94).

3. The right hand continues its travel down to the right knee as the left hand turns palm-up (rotating laterally) and arcs to the left side of the head. As the right hand passes the knee, the waist turns slightly right (bringing the left elbow forward) and the right foot twists on the heel so that the toe points out. At the same time, weight shifts completely to the right leg. Next, the left foot steps forward at a twenty-five-degree angle as the left hand begins to push forward from the shoulder (see figure 5.95).

## Movement #33: **Grasp and Hit** ***(Shen Xian Yi Bao Zhua)***

1. Simultaneously:
    - Weight shifts forward onto the left leg.

Figure 5.96a

Figure 5.96b

- Left hand becomes a fist as it arcs right, down, and left toward the left knee (the forearm crosses in front of the body).

- Right hand becomes a fist as it arcs back (rotating palm-up laterally) and up to the right side of the chest (see figures 5.96a and 5.96b).

2. Right hand punches forward (west) and down at a forty-five-degree angle as the left hand arcs around the left side of the body and behind the back (but not too far; it should not cross the spine). The body bends slightly forward at the *kua* as the right hand punches down. This movement is executed with *fa jin* (see figure 5.97).

Figure 5.97

## ✖ Movement #34: **Double Kick** *(Ti Er Qi)*

1. Right shoulder sinks forward slightly. Next, simultaneously:

   • The entire body quickly turns 180 degrees right as the left foot pivots on its heel.

   • Right elbow travels up and back, then around to the right at shoulder level (following the turning of the body). When it points east, it arcs down to the bottom of the right side of the rib cage as the back of the right fist comes down with force until it is slightly higher than the elbow.

   • Left hand unwinds from its position behind the back, then rises up (palm facing in) in front of the chest until the fist is at collarbone level and the elbow is bent.

   • Right foot retracts into a left-weighted, east-facing empty-stance (see figure 5.98).

2. Right fist arcs down, past the right hip (where it becomes an open palm), while the left hand becomes an open palm and begins to push straight forward from the shoulder (palm side leading). At the same time, the right foot steps forward with

Figure 5.98

Figure 5.99

the toe turned out. As weight moves forward onto the right leg, the right hand continues its travel back while the left hand continues to push forward (see figure 5.99).

3. Simultaneously:

   • Jump straight up (not forward) off the right leg as the left knee drives up hard and high.

   • Right hand arcs up and forward past the head, palm leading.

   • Left hand swings down to the left side (see figure 5.100).

4. Right foot snaps up with force as the right hand swings down, meeting the top of the foot with a sharp, audible slap. At the same time, the left foot begins its return to the ground (see figure 5.101).

*Figure 5.100*                              *Figure 5.101*

## ✖ Movement #35: **Protect the Heart Punch (Hu Xin Quan)**

1. Land in a left-weighted empty-stance. Right hand arcs down to the left side as weight sinks (see figures 5.102a and 5.102b).

2. Left hand turns palm-up (rotating laterally) as it arcs back, up to head level, then forward (east) until it is slightly forward of the body. The right hand turns palm-out (rotating medially) as it moves synchronously with the left and about a forearm's length in front (east) of it. Eyes follow hands (see figure 5.103).

*Figure 5.102a*

*Figure 5.102b*

*Figure 5.103*

3. Both hands continue their circle (wrists leading) in an east-west plane down to mid-chest level as the weight sinks. Next, the hands push quickly up as the right foot slide-steps straight right (south; see figure 5.104).

4. Both hands become fists. Then, simultaneously:

   • Weight shifts right and the waist turns toward the right knee.

   • Body bends deeply at the *kua* toward the right knee (as always, the spine remains perfectly straight).

   • Right elbow flexes and arcs toward the right knee, then below

Figure 5.104

Figure 5.105

it. At the same time, the left arm extends as the body moves away from it (see figure 5.105).

5. The waist continues its rightward turning as the right elbow continues around the right knee. At the same time, the left forearm begins to bend and arc over the head. As the right elbow returns toward the body (having circled the right knee), the torso begins to rise into a vertical position and the left forearm descends straight down in front of the head and chest. The torso finishes its straightening as the right elbow retracts to the bottom of the right side of the rib cage, with the forearm vertical and the palm facing in. At the same time, the left forearm continues its descent (remaining horizontal) until the left fist is under the right elbow. Next, the weight sinks (see figure 5.106).

6. Weight shifts quickly left, the waist snaps left (ends facing east), and the right fist

Figure 5.106

twists slightly inward, issuing force at chin level. This movement is executed with *fa jin* (see figures 5.107a and 5.107b).

*Figure 5.107a*    *Figure 5.107b*

## ✠ Movement #36: **Tornado Kick** *(Xuan Feng Jiao)*

1. Both hands become open palms and turn out (rotating medially). Weight shifts right as the right hand arcs up to head level, out, and right. At the same time, left hand arcs down and left. Weight then shifts left as the left hand turns palm-up (rotating laterally) while continuing its arc up; the right hand continues its arc down. Next, both hands converge, crossing in front of the chest (right palm up, left palm down) as the right foot swings in a circle up to the left, then to the right and back down to the ground, landing a shoulder's width east of the left foot. The right foot lands lightly on the heel, with the toe turned out (see figure 5.108).

2. Weight shifts forward onto the right leg as both palms turn out (see figure 5.109).

Figure 5.108

Figure 5.109

Figure 5.110

3. Body begins to turn right as the left foot (ankle flexed so that the heel protrudes) kicks high toward the east, beginning a 360-degree swing that will carry it all the way around the body. At the same time, both hands arc out at shoulder level with the palms leading. The left palm meets the left foot with an audible slap when both are extended straight east (see figure 5.110).

4. The left foot continues its swing around to the west as the body follows, pivoting on the right foot. At the same time, both hands lower from the shoulders so that the arms extend down and out from the body at about a thirty-degree angle. After the left foot returns to the ground about a shoulder's width west of the right, weight shifts left. Look right (see figure 5.111).

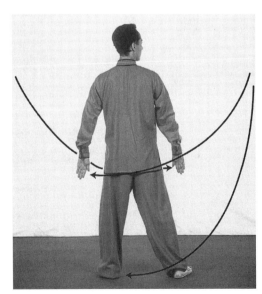

Figure 5.111

## ✳ Movement #37: **Right Heel Kick** *(You Deng Yi Gen)*

1. Open palms become fists as both hands come together in front of the navel with palms facing in. At the same time, the right foot rises as far as possible up and in toward the right hip into a "cocked" position with the ankle flexed (see figures 5.112a and 5.112b).

2. Right heel kicks straight right with force as both fists rise up and swing straight out at shoulder level. Right foot and left hand issue *fa jin* with equal force (see figure 5.113).

*Figure 5.112a*

*Figure 5.112b*

*Figure 5.113*

## ✳ Movement #38: **Covered Hand Punch** *(Yan Shou Hong Quan)*

1. Body turns right to face east as the right knee draws sharply in and up. At the same time, both hands become open palms, with the right hand chopping sharply down to the right side and the left hand swinging forward and up high. This movement is executed with *fa jin* (see figure 5.114).

2. Jump off the left foot and land with a stomp on the right. Weight immediately sinks, and the left foot steps forward at a forty-five-degree angle. At the same time, the hands come together to cross at the wrists, palm-down at diaphragm level with the left hand on top (see figure 5.115).

*Figure 5.114*            *Figure 5.115*

3. Repeat Movement #14, steps (2) and (3).

## ✕ Movement #39: **Small Catch and Hit (Xiao Qin Da)**

1. Right hand becomes open palm (facing down). Weight shifts completely to the left leg as the left toe turns out. Next, the right foot steps forward at a twenty-five-degree angle (see figure 5.116).

2. Weight shifts forward onto the right leg as the body and right foot turn right. Next, the left foot steps forward at a fifteen-degree angle (fifteen degrees north of east). As the body moves forward (during the step), the right hand stays in place and

sinks a few inches lower so that the body catches up to it. At the same time, the left hand arcs forward, up, and down (palm leading) in front of the right (see figure 5.117).

Figure 5.116

Figure 5.117

3. Without changing orientation, both hands push straight forward as weight shifts forward onto the left leg. Both hands then arc up and back to the right: left hand turns palm-back and goes a bit higher than the top of the head, while the right hand flexes up at the wrist (so that the palm faces forward) and stays below and just inside the left elbow. At the same time, weight shifts back to the right leg, and the waist turns a bit farther to the right (torso faces just slightly west of south). Weight and *dan tian* sink. Eyes continue to look east throughout this movement (see figure 5.118).

4. Weight shifts left, and the waist makes a short leftward snap as the left arm issues force to the east. Right hand maintains its position relative to the left elbow. This movement is executed with *fa jin* (see figure 5.119).

| *Figure 5.118* | *Figure 5.119* | *Figure 5.120* |

5. Right foot withdraws straight toward the left into a left-weighted empty-stance. At the same time, the right hand issues very short force to the left. In doing so, it does not pass beyond the outside of the left elbow. This movement is executed with *fa jin* (see figure 5.120).

## ✖ Movement #40: **Embrace Head, Push Mountain** *(Bao Tou Tui Shan)*

1. Body and left foot turn right into a west-facing empty-stance as weight sinks and the left forearm tips in to cross inside the right. When the body faces west, weight sinks low and both hands "scissor" down in front of the right knee (see figure 5.121).

2. Weight rises slightly on the left leg as the torso turns left. At the same

*Figure 5.121*

time, the hands separate, opening wide to the sides. Look left. As the right foot steps forward at a fifteen-degree angle, the hands rotate laterally palm-up and continue their arc out, up, and in to the sides of the head. They end with the fingers pointing in toward the head, and the elbows pointing out. The shoulders are slightly back so that the chest is open (see figure 5.122).

3. As weight shifts forward onto the right leg, the waist turns right (torso ends facing west) and the hands push straight forward from the head while the elbows rotate down and the chest closes (see figure 5.123).

Figure 5.122    Figure 5.123

## ✕ Movement #41: **Six Sealing, Four Closing (Liu Feng Si Bi)**

Repeat Movement #4, steps (2) and (3).

## ✕ Movement #42: **Single Whip (Dan Bian)**

Repeat Movement #5.

# �֎ Movement #43: **Forward Technique (Qian Zhao)**

1. Right hand becomes open palm and arcs down and in toward the abdomen while the palm turns in (see figure 5.124).

*Figure 5.124*

2. Right hand continues its arc to the left side of the abdomen. As the body turns ninety degrees right and weight shifts to the right foot, the right hand continues up to the left shoulder, then (rotating palm-out medially) out and forward (west) at head level. At the same time, the left hand arcs down toward the left thigh with the palm leading (see figure 5.125).

3. Both hands continue their travel as the left foot steps forward at a twenty-five-degree angle: right hand arcs out to the right while the left hand arcs up to the right side of the chest. At the same time, the waist turns slightly right. Eyes watch the right hand (see figures 5.126a and 5.126b).

*Figure 5.125*

*Figure 5.126a*

*Figure 5.126b*

4. Weight shifts forward onto the left leg as the hands continue to move: the right hand goes down to hip level and across toward the left, while the left hand turns palm-out and goes up, out (away from the body), and toward the left. At the same time, the waist turns slightly left. As soon as weight is on the left foot, the right foot steps quickly forward into a left-weighted empty-stance, and both hands end their travel by issuing force to the left. The left arm ends with the elbow pointing slightly forward of left and the palm facing left. The right hand ends below the left, with the palm parallel to the outside of the left hip. Eyes watch the left hand. This movement is executed with *fa jin* (see figure 5.127).

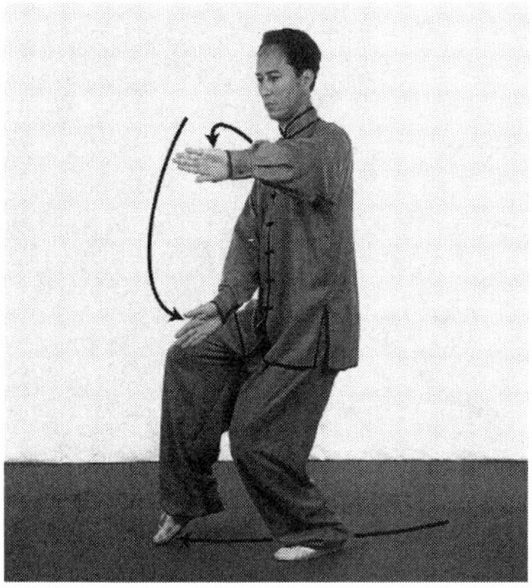

*Figure 5.127*

## ⌘ Movement #44: **Backward Technique *(Hou Zhao)***

1. Right hand arcs up to the left shoulder where it turns palm-out, then continues its travel out and right at shoulder level. At the same time, the left hand arcs left, down to hip level and right, and the waist turns slightly right. Both hands end their travel by issuing force to the right.

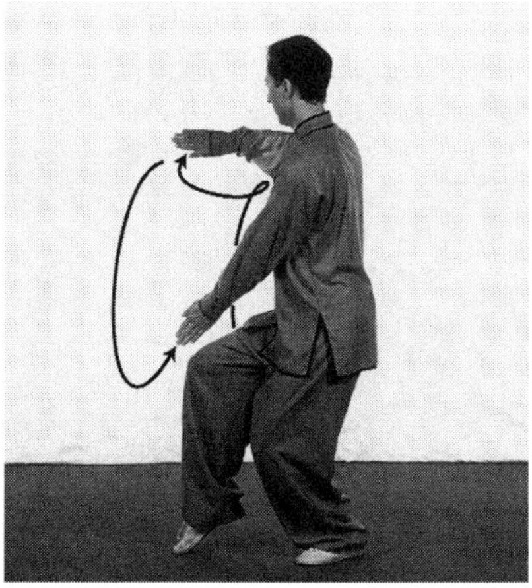

*Figure 5.128*

The position of the hands is a mirror image of their position at the end of Movement #43. Eyes watch the right hand. This movement is executed with *fa jin* (see figure 5.128).

## ❖ Movement #45: **Part the Mustang's Mane** *(Ye Ma Fen Zong)*

1. Both hands turn palm-down and arc down and back to the left with the left hand leading. When the right hand reaches the left side of the waist, it travels up to the left shoulder as the left hand continues back to nearly full extension, then (rotating palm-up laterally) up past shoulder level. Eyes look back at the left hand as the right foot steps straight west (see figure 5.129).

2. Eyes look forward (west) as the right hand turns palm-out (rotating medially). Weight shifts forward onto the right foot as the body turns right and both hands begin to arc up. Left foot takes a large step forward (west) at a twenty-degree angle as the left hand arcs up high overhead and the right hand arcs up to the left side of the face. As weight continues forward onto

Figure 5.129

Figure 5.130

the left leg, both hands continue forward and down: the left hand extending straight ahead, the right hand close to the inside of the left elbow (see figure 5.130).

3. Weight shifts back to the right leg, the waist turns slightly right, and weight sinks low. At the same time, both hands pull down and back to the right, maintaining their relative separation. As the right hand passes the right hip and rotates palm-up laterally, the left hand begins to travel up toward the right shoulder. Eyes watch the right hand (see figures 5.131a and 5.131b).

4. Left hand turns palm-out as eyes look west. Weight shifts forward onto the left leg as the body turns left and both hands arc up and forward: right hand goes high overhead while the left hand goes forward past the right side of the face (both palms leading). When weight is on the left leg, the waist turns left and the right foot steps straight forward (west). Both hands continue their paths forward as weight shifts to the right leg (see figure 5.132).

*Figure 5.131a*  *Figure 5.131b*  *Figure 5.132*

## ✖ Movement #46: **Six Sealing, Four Closing** *(Liu Feng Si Bi)*

Repeat Movement #4, steps (2) and (3).

## ✖ Movement #47: **Single Whip** *(Dan Bian)*

Repeat Movement #5.

## ✖ Movement #48: **Jade Maiden Works Shuttles** *(Yu Nü Chuan Suo)*

1. Quickly and simultaneously:

   • Body turns right (faces west) as weight shifts completely to the left leg and the right foot withdraws into a left-weighted empty-stance.

   • Right hand becomes an open palm and makes a very small, clockwise semi-circle—down, left, and up—while with-drawing slightly closer to the body. It ends with the palm facing left and the fingertips at collarbone level.

   • Left hand moves directly to a position near the lower part of the right forearm. The left palm faces right, and both hands are lined up on an east-west axis (see figure 5.133).

2. Weight and wrists sink quickly. Next, jump straight up off the left

*Figure 5.133*

*Figure 5.134*    *Figure 5.135*    *Figure 5.136*

leg as the right knee lifts up and both wrists rise (see figure 5.134).

3. As the wrists sink down, the left foot lands first, then the right. Both feet stomp flat on the ground, but weight remains on the left leg (see figure 5.135).

4. Right knee rises up with the ankle flexed while both hands withdraw straight in, close to the chest (see figure 5.136).

5. Right foot kicks straight forward at hip level with the heel leading. At the same time, the right palm pushes straight forward (parallel to the right leg) and the left elbow goes straight back. Right foot and left elbow issue equal force. This movement is executed with *fa jin* (see figure 5.137).

6. Right foot takes a large step forward as it returns to the ground. Weight drives forward off the left leg and onto the right. When weight is on the right leg, simultaneously:

   • Leap forward as far as you can off the right leg as the left foot swings forward and the body rotates about ninety degrees right.

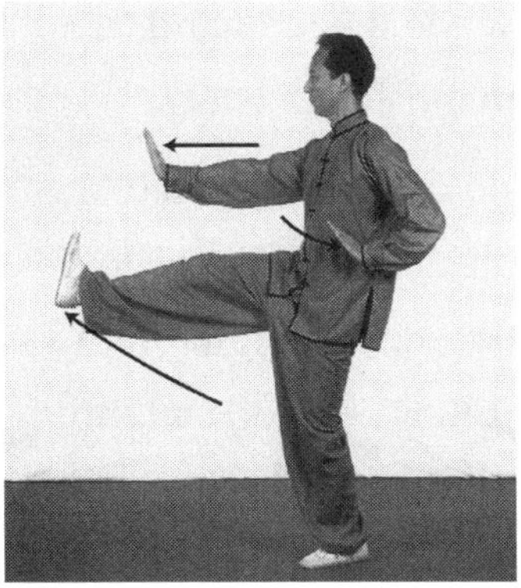
Figure 5.137

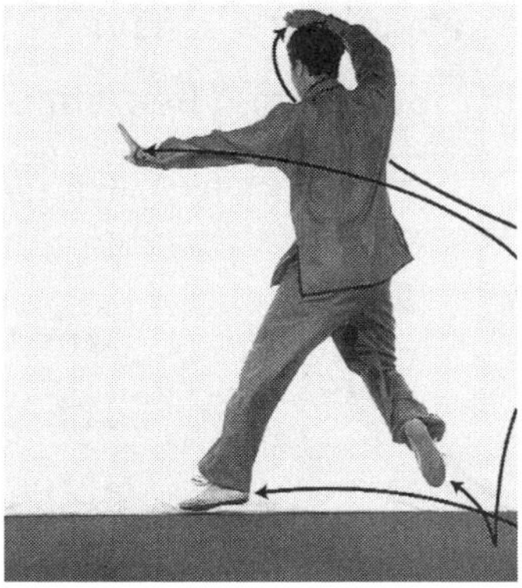
Figure 5.138

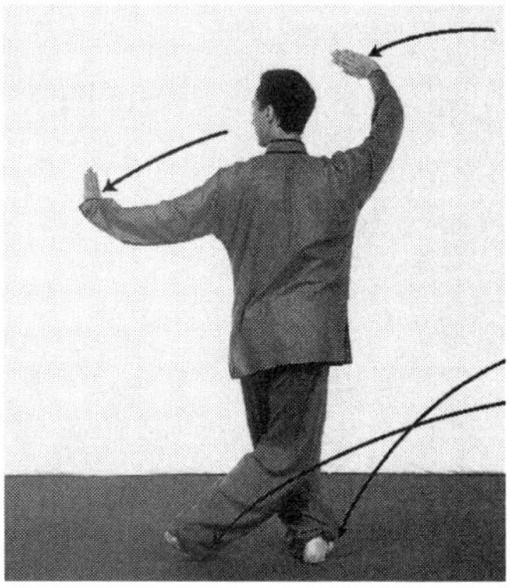
Figure 5.139

- Left palm drives straight forward to nearly full extension while issuing force.
- Right hand arcs up to a position in front of and slightly above the forehead (see figure 5.138).

7. Left foot lands with toe pointing north (weight is balanced). Right foot steps lightly behind the left into a resting stance (see figure 5.139).

## Movement #49: **Lazily Tucking Clothes *(Lan Zha Yi)***

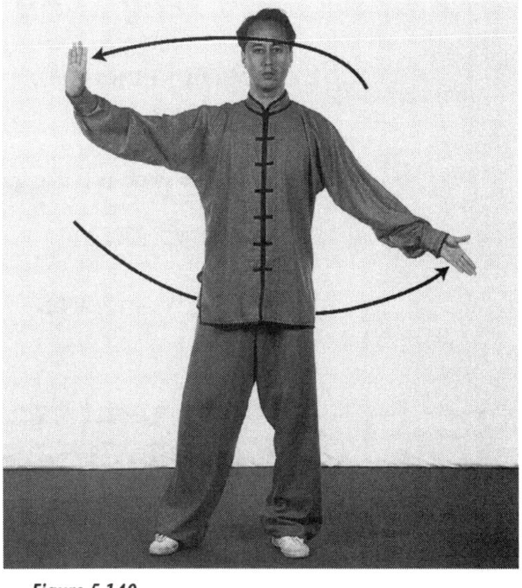
Figure 5.140

1. Body and feet turn 180 degrees right. Left hand follows the turning of the body, arcing east, while the right hand extends and arcs west. Weight remains on the left leg (see figure 5.140).
2. Both hands continue their arcs: the

right hand travels down, left, and up, while the left hand travels up, right, and down. Then, simultaneously:

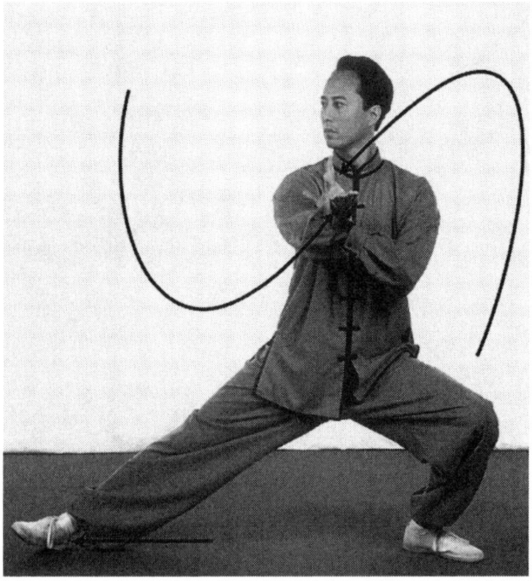
*Figure 5.141*

- Hands end crossed in front of the chest with the left wrist or forearm resting on the right elbow. The right hand extends slightly away from the body as it crosses with the left. The right palm now faces up, and the left palm faces right or down.
- Weight sinks on the left leg, and the right foot slide-steps right.
- Eyes look right (see figure 5.141).

3. Repeat Movement #3, step (4).

## ⌘ Movement #50: **Six Sealing, Four Closing *(Liu Feng Si Bi)***

Repeat Movement #4.

## ⌘ Movement #51: **Single Whip *(Dan Bian)***

Repeat Movement #5.

## ⌘ Movement #52: **Hand Technique *(Yun Shou)***

Repeat Movement #27.

# ✠ Movement #53: **Swing Foot** *(Bai Jiao)*

1. Simultaneously:

   - Look left.

   - Left hand rotates palm-down and pushes a forearm's length left of the left side of the waist.

   - Right hand rotates palm-down and arcs down, past the navel, and toward the left side of the waist.

   - Weight shifts left, then the right foot steps to a position immediately adjacent to the left foot (see figure 5.142).

2. Left hand turns palm-up (rotating laterally) as the right hand turns palm-out (rotating medially). At the same time, both hands (maintaining their relative separation) arc up to head level as the left foot steps east at a fifteen-degree angle. As weight shifts left and the body and hips turn left into a front bow-stance, the right hand arcs back to nearly full extension (rotating palm-out laterally) and down to hip level, while the left hand arcs past the right shoulder and down to diaphragm level. Eyes look east (see figure 5.143).

*Figure 5.142*

*Figure 5.143*

*Figure 5.144*

*Figure 5.145*

3. Right foot sweeps forward and up to the left (but does not fully extend) as both hands begin to move forward. As the right foot continues its arc to the right, the left hand (moving right to left) slaps it on top (see figure 5.144).

4. Right foot continues its travel to the right and back (with the knee staying bent). When it reaches the right side of the body, the right hand slaps it on the side, using a short forward movement. The right leg exerts maximum force in the last part of this movement. At the same time, the left hand follows through by moving slightly left (see figure 5.145).

## ✕ Movement #54: **Drop and Split** *(Die Cha)*

1. Right leg relaxes (but the knee stays up). Forearms cross in front of the diaphragm: right arm arcing left and up, and left arm arcing right and down (see figure 5.146).

2. Jump up off the left leg and land on the right foot with a stomp. Next, the left heel slides forward (east) as weight descends all

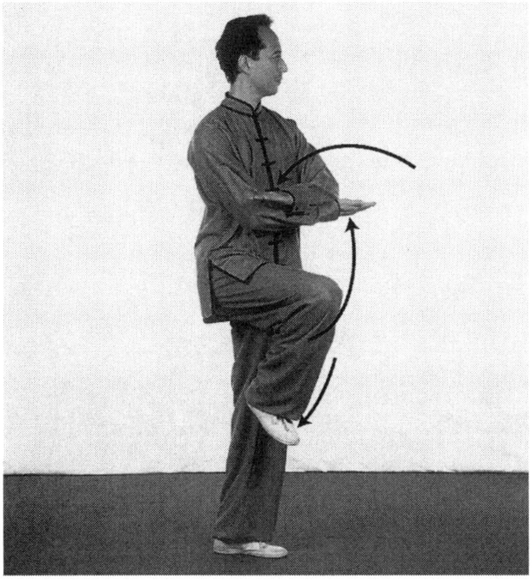

*Figure 5.146*

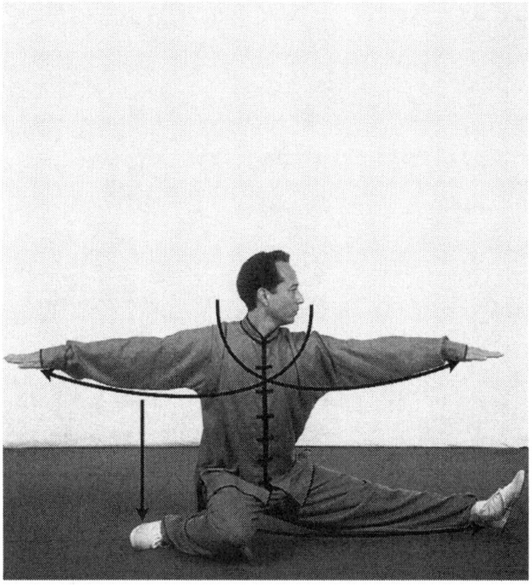

*Figure 5.147*

the way down into a right-weighted split-stance. As the weight descends, the right palm turns down and both arms open straight out from the shoulders. Right arm ends pointing west and left arm ends pointing east (see figure 5.147).

When performing this movement, it is essential that the back remain perfectly vertical. If the legs and hips are not strong enough to maintain correct posture, then it is permissible to stop descending at a higher point in the stance.

## ⌘ Movement #55: Golden Rooster Stands on One Leg *(Jin Zhi Du Li)*

1. Push up and forward off the right leg into a left-weighted, front bow-stance (facing east). At the same time, the left hand descends to the left side and the right hand arcs down beside the right thigh. The right foot steps forward into a left-weighted

Figure 5.148a                    Figure 5.148b

empty-stance while the right hand follows, maintaining its position close to the right thigh (see figures 5.148a and 5.148b).

2. Right hand lifts straight up to collarbone level, where it rotates medially (so that the fingers point back) then pushes straight up above the shoulder. At the same time, the left hand pushes straight down at the left side, the right knee rises, and the *dan tian* moves back toward the spine. Right foot ends with the toe pointed in front of the left kneecap (see figure 5.149).

3. Right hand descends to the right side (palm-down) as the right foot returns to the ground with a stomp. Feet are shoulder-width apart, and weight remains mostly on the left leg (see figure 5.150).

4. Right hand moves slightly right and left hand moves slightly left. Next, the right hand pushes quickly to the left at abdomen level (palm leading), while the right foot slides right on the ball of the foot (the heel is just slightly off the ground). When the right hand reaches the left side of the waist, both hands issue force (with *fa jin*) to the left, while the right foot stops

*Figure 5.149*        *Figure 5.150*

abruptly on the heel (the whole foot is on the ground, but heel pressure causes the foot to stop). Eyes watch the right hand (see figure 5.151).

5. Weight shifts right as the right hand turns palm-down and arcs to the side of the right hip. At the same time, the left hand turns palm-up and moves next to the left thigh, then follows as the left foot moves right into a right-weighted empty-stance (see figure 5.152).

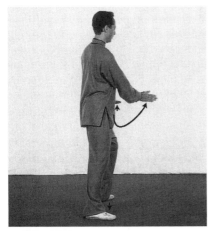
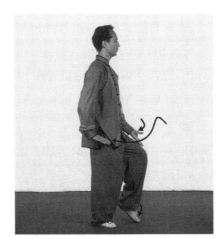

*Figure 5.151*        *Figure 5.152*

*Figure 5.153*

6. Left hand lifts straight up to collarbone level, where it rotates medially (so that the fingers point back) then pushes straight up above the shoulder. At the same time, the right hand pushes straight down at the right side, the left knee rises, and the *dan tian* moves back toward the spine. Left foot ends with the toe pointed in front of the right kneecap (see figure 5.153).

## ⋈ Movement #56: Step Back and Swing Arms (*Dao Nian Hong*)

1. The left hand arcs forward and down past the left knee, while the right hand arcs back (rotating palm-up laterally) and up to the right side of the neck (see figure 5.154).

2. Repeat Movement #20, steps (2)–(5).

*Figure 5.154*

## ✖ Movement #57: **White Goose Spreads Wings (Bai E Liang Chi)**

Repeat Movement #21.

## ✖ Movement #58: **Oblique Posture (Xie Xing)**

Repeat Movement #22.

## ✖ Movement #59: **Flash the Back (Shan Tong Bei)**

Repeat Movement #23.

## ✖ Movement #60: **Covered Hand Punch (Yan Shou Hong Quan)**

Repeat Movement #24.

## ✖ Movement #61: **Six Sealing, Four Closing (Liu Feng Si Bi)**

Repeat Movement #25.

## ✖ Movement #62: **Single Whip (Dan Bian)**

Repeat Movement #26.

## ✖ Movement #63: **Hand Technique (Yun Shou)**

Repeat Movement #27.

## ✖ Movement #64: **High Pat on Horse** *(Gao Tan Ma)*

Repeat Movement #28.

## ✖ Movement #65: **Cross Foot** *(Shi Zi Jiao)*

1. Right hand rotates so that fingers point east, and it pushes slightly forward (see figures 5.155a and 5.155b).

*Figure 5.155a*          *Figure 5.155b*

2. Left wrist pivots to the right around the fingertips, while the right wrist rotates down and right (see figures 5.156a and 5.156b).

3. Body and right foot turn 180 degrees right as weight sinks low and the left foot slide-steps directly east of the right foot. As the foot steps, the left hand follows the turning of the body then pushes toward a point above the left knee. At the same time, the right hand arcs up and right past the head (see figure 5.157).

4. Weight shifts to the left foot as the left hand turns palm-up laterally and arcs high above the left shoulder. At the same time, the right hand arcs down in front of the right thigh. Next, the

Figure 5.156a        Figure 5.156b        Figure 5.157

body turns ninety degrees right as the right foot withdraws into a left-weighted empty-stance (facing west). The left arm follows the turning of the body, then the left elbow sinks straight down to lower chest level as the right hand arcs up just underneath it. The right palm faces in and the left palm faces right. Sink the *dan tian* and weight (see figure 5.158).

5. Right foot swings in an arc up to the left, then right (knee stays bent). Left hand swings down to slap the top of the right foot as the foot swings right. At the same time, the right hand swings up high to the right (see figure 5.159).

Figure 5.158        Figure 5.159

## ✖ Movement #66: **Groin Punch** *(Zhi Dang Chui)*

1. The right hand chops straight down to the right side as the left hand swings up high above and in front of the left shoulder (see figure 5.160).

2. Jump straight up off the left leg and land on the right foot with a stomp. Waist turns slightly right. At the same time, weight sinks onto the right leg as the left foot steps forward at a forty-five-degree angle and the left hand arcs down to mid-chest level (see figure 5.161).

3. Weight shifts forward onto the left leg. At the same time, the right hand becomes a fist as it arcs back and up to the right side of the chest, and the left hand arcs down to the right. Next, the waist rotates left as the right hand punches forward and down at a fifty-degree angle while the left elbow pulls left in front of the waist. The left hand ends resting on the left hip. This movement is executed with *fa jin* (see figure 5.162).

*Figure 5.160*       *Figure 5.161*       *Figure 5.162*

# ✖ Movement #67: **Monkey Picks Fruit** *(Yuan Hou Tan Guo)*

This movement is sometimes called "White Ape Offers Fruit" *(Bai Yuan Tan Guo)*.

1. Right shoulder sinks forward and down slightly as the right fist curls down and left. Right hand continues toward the left hip as the body turns ninety degrees left and the right foot steps straight west of the left foot. Eyes follow the right hand (see figure 5.163).

2. The right hand continues up to the right shoulder as the left hand arcs left and up (rotating palm-up laterally) to head level (see figure 5.164).

*Figure 5.163*          *Figure 5.164*

3. The right fist becomes an open palm and rotates palm-out medially as the left hand continues to the left side of the neck. Eyes look forty-five degrees right. Then, simultaneously:

   • Weight shifts to the right foot as the waist turns slightly right (the torso should face about twenty degrees west of south).

*Figure 5.165*

Left foot steps to the right, ending in a south-facing, right-weighted empty-stance.

- Both hands push forward at a forty-five-degree angle to the right while both elbows rotate down, but not all the way. Hands end at mid-chest level, the right slightly higher than the left, and elbows are moderately bent. The right elbow is slightly more extended than the left.

Sink the *dan tian* and weight onto the right leg as the hands complete their travel (see figure 5.165).

## ✖ Movement #68: **Single Whip (Dan Bian)**

Repeat Movement #5.

## ✖ Movement #69: **Dragon Hacks the Ground (Qie Di Long)**

1. Both hands become fists. Weight shifts left and the body turns ninety degrees left. At the same time, the left hand goes to the right shoulder (palm facing left) while the right hand arcs down and left, ending extended and palm-up at waist level (see figure 5.166).

2. Simultaneously:

    - Weight shifts onto the right leg and descends into a right-weighted split-stance.

*Figure 5.166*

*Figure 5.167*

- Right hand arcs up and back past the head, ending high and forty-five degrees right of the right shoulder, with the fist curled slightly in.

- Left fist travels down to the top of the left thigh, then extends along the thigh toward the knee. The palm is up (see figure 5.167).

As with Movement #54, it is essential that the back remain perfectly vertical in the end posture.

## ✖ Movement #70: **Step Up, Make Seven Stars *(Shang Bu Qi Xing)***

1. Push up and forward off the right foot into a left-weighted, front bow-stance. At the same time, the left fist pushes forward and rises to mid-chest level as the right fist arcs down and in toward the left side of the waist, where it rests palm-up (see figure 5.168).

Figure 5.168                    Figure 5.169

2. As the right foot steps forward into a left-weighted empty-stance, the right fist rotates palm-left and pushes straight forward at diaphragm level until it is forward of the right knee. At the same time, the left fist rotates palm-right (see figure 5.169).

3. Both hands become open palm. The right hand arcs up to nose level while the left hand arcs slightly down, then out. At the same time, weight rises. The right hand continues its travel in as the left hand continues up, then in to cross with the right at the wrist (right wrist is inside). At this point, hands sink to mid-chest level as weight and *dan tian* also sink (see figure 5.170).

4. Hands, weight, and *dan tian* sink again. Then, in one swift motion with hands remaining connected at the wrist: hands drop slightly below the elbows (with the palms down); hands "scissor" in toward the body so that the left wrist pivots to the top; hands continue their circle up, passing close to the chest (right hand is now inside); hands continue their circle out and slightly down, ending where they started, but with the palms facing in. The *dan tian* leads the motion of the hands throughout

Figure 5.170

Figure 5.171

this step, making a vertical circle perpendicular to the plane of the body (see figure 5.171).

## ✖ Movement #71: Step Back, Open Arms (*Xia Bu Kua Hong*)

1. Right foot steps back at a twenty-degree angle. As weight shifts back to the right leg, the right hand rotates palm-down and arcs down past the right hip (see figure 5.172).

2. Body and feet turn about 130 degrees right. Left foot takes a small step to the southwest of the right and rests lightly on its heel.

Figure 5.172

*Figure 5.173*

*Figure 5.174*

The right hand turns palm-up, and the arms cross at the forearm in front of the lower chest (see figure 5.173).

3. Body and feet turn right to face north. At the same time, the right hand turns palm-out and arcs up and right at head level, while the left hand arcs down and left to the outside of the left hip (see figure 5.174).

4. Left foot steps forward at a twenty-five-degree angle (twenty-five degrees west of north). At the same time, the right hand continues its arc to collarbone level and right as the left hand rotates palm-up laterally and continues up to collarbone level and right. Hands end a forearm's length apart in front of the chest, and the arms are bent (see figure 5.175).

5. Weight shifts completely to the left leg. The entire body pivots 180 degrees around the left foot as the right foot steps backward to a position twenty-five degrees west of north from the left foot. Both hands follow, maintaining their relative positions. Weight shifts back to the right leg (see figure 5.176).

Figure 5.175

Figure 5.176

6. Both hands begin to arc back and down. Then, simultaneously:

- Weight shifts forward onto the left leg.

- Right hand continues its arc back to the right and down, ending extended at hip level with the palm facing up or out.

- Left hand arcs right, past the right shoulder, and down to diaphragm level. When the forearm is horizontal, the left elbow moves straight forward, parallel to the plane of the body (see figure 5.177).

Figure 5.177

## ✖ Movement #72: Swing Foot (Bai Jiao)

Repeat Movement #53, steps (3) and (4).

## ✖ Movement #73: **Head-on Cannon** (*Dang Men Pao*)

*Figure 5.178*

1. Both hands reach slightly high and thirty degrees to the left as the right foot steps back at a twenty-five-degree angle (see figure 5.178).

2. As weight shifts back to the right leg, the waist turns right. At the same time, both hands make fists and pull down to the right side of the waist, where they both turn palm-up. Eyes continue to look south (see figures 5.179a and 5.179b).

3. Weight shifts forward onto the left leg as the waist turns left and both hands punch forward. The hands follow the turning of the body as they do this, so that their paths are curved. The left hand ends with the wrist as far forward as the left toe, and the right hand ends with the knuckles as far forward as the left knee. This movement is executed with *fa jin* (see figure 5.180).

*Figure 5.179a*         *Figure 5.179b*         *Figure 5.180*

## ✖ Movement #74: **Diamond King Pounds Mortar (*Jin Gang Dao Dui*)**

1. Weight and *dan tian* sink. Both hands become open palms as the right hand turns palm-out. Weight shifts back to the right leg and the waist turns right as both hands arc up to collarbone level and back (see figure 5.181).

2. Both hands continue to arc back and down until they are at diaphragm level. Then, simultaneously:

   • Weight shifts forward onto the left leg.

   • Right hand continues its arc back to the right and down, ending extended at hip level with the palm facing up or out.

   • Left elbow moves straight forward at diaphragm level, parallel to the plane of the body (see figure 5.182).

3. Repeat Movement #2, steps (6)–(9).

Figure 5.181

Figure 5.182

## ✵ Movement #75: **Closing Movement** *(Shou Shi)*

1. Weight shifts to the right leg, left foot takes a small step left, and the stance becomes a horse stance. Weight and *dan tian* sink as the right fist becomes open palm (palm faces up) and both hands separate to the sides with the wrists leading (see figure 5.183).

*Figure 5.183*    *Figure 5.184*    *Figure 5.185*

2. Weight rises as both hands rotate laterally (palms lead throughout this movement) and continue their arcs out, up to head level, and in. The right hand pushes straight down to waist level in front of the right side of the torso, while the left hand does the same on the left side. Weight sinks as the hands push down (see figure 5.184).

3. Weight slowly rises as the hands relax at the sides (see figure 5.185).

Chapter 6

# Training with an Opponent

## ⌘ 6.1 Push-Hands

"Push-hands" *(tui shou),* Taiji's rhythmic, two-person training, is as puzzling to most students as it is to observers.

My first Taiji instructor drilled me extensively in a variety of push-hands exercises. I knew that these were somehow related to combat training, but for many years, I had no idea how. After my teacher's death, I visited various Taiji schools in the hope of continuing my education, and when instructors offered to try push-hands with me, I was always happy to oblige. Sometimes I would get attacked in the midst of these sessions and, if the instructor was skilled, I would fall down. If the instructor was not skilled, I would generally fall down anyway (it only seemed polite). Push-hands, I concluded, was a sort of ritual Taiji greeting: the host does a few circles with the guest, then shoves him to the floor.

The only type of push-hands I had known—the only type known to most Taijiquan practitioners—was a simple, repetitive drill performed in contact with a partner. In the most elementary of these exercises, the partners face each other, make contact at the wrist, and simply move their hands back and forth in a circle. And if this is all that happens, then push-hands is indeed quite pointless (perhaps why bogus Taiji schools often advertise it as an exercise in "interpersonal harmony" or the like).

Push-hands is, in fact, combat training. Like every other Taijiquan exercise, its purpose (as the attentive reader has already divined) is to train deep coordination and coherent movement. We use solo forms to train the fundamentals of these principles, and we use push-hands to train their application: how to stay connected and move coherently while external forces are applied to the body. In directing force at the opponent, we learn to find the opponent's "center" (the vector where our attack cannot be redirected) and to follow it as it moves; when receiving an incoming force, we "listen" to it *(ting jin)*, interpret it *(dong jin)*, and neutralize it *(zhou hua)*. These skills are employed continuously in any engagement, and the processes that implement them must reside deeper in consciousness than deliberate cognition. Think of sitting in a chair. You do not sit in the chair then calculate precisely where to shift your limbs in order to be comfortable; you simply have a feeling inside of what "comfortable" is, and you allow your body to conform to it. This analogy is actually quite close to the subjective experience of applying Taiji. If you train correctly, then "comfortable" will mean that your body mechanics are correct, and you are moving coherently in response to the opponent's force.

A critical failing of many martial-arts systems is that they treat engagements as sequences of discrete events. Techniques are practiced individually; one student initiates, the other responds, then the tableau is reset and the scene repeated. Trained in this way, students never learn to function in a continuum. In a real fight, the martial artist must find entry to her attack or counter-attack while a lot of different things are moving at once. She does not get a chance to stop and reset if a technique fails. And if it succeeds, she may still lose if she emerges at the end in a compromised position, or if she fails to press her advantage (opponents often do not respond as expected). Successful advances may create small breaks in the opponent's structure that must be precisely and instantly exploited in order to achieve a decisive outcome. Final success often results from accumulation of several small advantages.

For these reasons, Taiji applications are usually practiced within the framework of push-hands. The student is thus forced to find entry for her technique in the midst of a moving situation, to execute the technique while following the opponent's force, and to exit the technique without compromising her own structure (this, of course, is the definition of coherent movement). At any point in this process, she must be able to alter her action freely in response to the opponent's changes. In this sense, techniques are not actually complete units, but vectors that are introduced and continuously augmented by both opponents in a variety of ways. Any break or discontinuity in the augmentation process creates a momentary void that a skilled practitioner can exploit as an entry (this is why continuity is stressed in forms practice). This is very different from the "set up—commit to attack—hope for the best" procedure used in the discrete-event type of training.

Push-hands is combat training, not combat. Even among Taiji schools that are astute enough to know that push-hands has a martial function, it is common to find a problem that I call the "fixed-step fetish": treating elementary-level push-hands exercises as if they were a meaningful skill in themselves, rather than a learning tool. This problem is usually the result of an incomplete curriculum. The instructor (or instructor's instructor, or school founder) was trained in some push-hands, but not enough to acquire a practical view of the system's objectives. As a result, students at these schools are frequently seen wrestling each other into strange contortions, all in an effort to avoid moving their feet—which, according to their rules, constitutes a "loss." Push-hands tournaments may have more or less liberal rules, but they generally suffer the same failing.

Students should therefore keep firmly in mind the fact that the outcome of any particular push-hands engagement is not indicative of either party's skill level. Push-hands exercises are designed to be limited in order to focus training on specific aspects of body mechanics. It is entirely possible to prevail in a push-hands engagement without having any meaningful martial-art skill; in fact, it is possible to prevail in a push-hands engagement precisely *because* of a lack of martial-art skill. Early and intermediate stages of push-hands training are largely about losing bad somatic habits. There is a long, dry stretch in this learning cycle where the student is trying to relax and avoid using stiff force (or "stupid force," as it is sometimes called) but has not yet learned to how to neutralize. During this phase, it is quite easy for any feckless clod to step in and prevail. If our diligent student remains unconcerned about getting shoved around by this less-skilled opponent, he will learn important lessons from every encounter. This is called "investing in loss."

Beginning push-hands exercises are mostly (not completely) cooperative. Students learn various patterns of movement (such as the simple, circular drill described above) and repeat these patterns while maintaining continuous contact. As the student advances, she graduates to exercises that are both more complex and less cooperative until, at the most advanced stage, "push-hands" becomes free-fighting *(san shou)*. Even in the simplest of these exercises, however, much more is going on than meets the eye.

In the traditional curriculum, push-hands training generally begins fairly late so that students develop good fundamentals before trying to cope with force. I prefer to start my students on push-hands training rather early—usually within their first couple of months of study. It takes a good deal of habituation for most people to maintain equanimity while being pushed or grappled, and there is no reason to delay this habituation process once the basic stances and alignments are understood. It is the instructor's job to prevent the development of bad habits.

You should practice push-hands as much as possible, with as many different partners as possible; however, when practicing with strangers or with students from other Taiji schools, it makes sense to clarify the ground rules before actually crossing hands. I have been elbowed, chopped, and kicked in many encounters that I believed to be friendly practice sessions. If your opponent is from a school that indulges in the fixed-step fetish, then you may find yourself engaged in a contortion contest against a person whose self-esteem desperately depends on making you move your feet. Do not play this game. Simply maintain correct structure and analyze what you have learned each time you get pushed back (pushing you back is usually all that the fixed-steppers know how to do). Your objective is to learn, not to win.

## Principles of Push-Hands Practice

In addition to the basic principles of coherent movement discussed above and throughout this book, there are several tactical issues that are important to the practice of push-hands (and, indeed, to Taiji combat):

• Use very light energy when first making contact with an opponent. *Dong jin* is one of the most important skills that you are trying to develop, and heavy hands make this impossible.

• Do not anticipate; *neutralize*. If advancing into the opponent, do not withdraw until the opponent begins to turn you back. The instant in which the opponent's intention changes, you must also change, but not before. This is the meaning of Wu Yu Xiang's, "My opponent is still, I am still; my opponent moves, I move first." In repetitive-pattern practice (in other words, beginning push-hands), anticipation completely abrogates the function of the exercise: you are simply moving in circles without actually connecting with the opponent. This defect can usually be felt as a change in pressure at the point of contact.

• Do not break contact. The "Song of Push-Hands" (attributed to Wang Zong Yue) preaches, *"zhan, lian, nian, sui."* Most translators try to attach individual English meanings to these words, but there is no accurate way to do it. Each word encompasses some combination of the meanings "contact, adhere, follow."

• Do not oppose force with force. One of Taiji's central tactics (again, laid down in the "Song of Push-Hands") is "leading into emptiness" *(yin kong).* Draw out your opponent's energy and redirect it so that the opponent becomes overextended. At this point, you may issue force to unbalance him.

It is worth mentioning here that a "push" in Taiji does not specifically mean a push; it is actually a generic way to indicate any type of force (which is why I use the latter term). Whether the force enters quickly (as with a punch) or slowly (as with a push), we connect and neutralize it in the same way. The speed of neutralization matches the speed of the attack.

In early stages of push-hands practice, you should not attempt any overtly adversarial techniques. If you do, you will develop wrestling habits rather than Taiji skills. You should instead concentrate on remaining completely relaxed and moving with correct body mechanics. If you pay careful attention, your partner will serve as a feedback mechanism, informing you of flaws in your movement. For example, a change in pressure at any contact point means that you have failed to follow your partner's force. A feeling of discomfort usually means that your structure is broken, and you must discover why. Tired arms or shoulders mean that you are stiff and not moving coherently. A feeling of imbalance means that your alignment is incorrect; your weight is shifting outside the geometry allowed by your stance, your lower back is arched, or your *kua* is not sunk. In every case, the defect must be sought and corrected.

## Fixed Step

The sequence presented here is actually one of the more complex push-hands exercises. The hand positions and basic dynamics of this exercise form the basis of the advanced exercises presented later, so the student is advised to study them thoroughly.

1. Grey and Black face each other squarely with their feet together. Both extend their arms at shoulder level so that their fists touch

(this gives them the proper spacing). Next, they both step forward with the right foot (either foot may be used, but our example uses the right) as if entering a front bow-stance (see section 4.4). The right feet should be side by side, about eight to twelve inches apart. Both partners shift their weight halfway forward as Grey partially extends his right hand at throat level and places his left hand inside the right elbow. At the same time, Black's right wrist connects with Grey's right wrist (ulna side), and Black's left hand touches the outside of Grey's right elbow (see figure 6.1).

*Figure 6.1*

*Figure 6.2*

2. Black's weight shifts forward as Grey's weight shifts back. At the same time, Black pushes down toward the left side of Grey's chest with his right hand as Black's left hand rolls over top of Grey's right elbow, onto Grey's left hand. Grey's right hand follows Black's right hand, arcing down to Grey's left elbow (see figure 6.2).

Grey must be careful that his right elbow does not travel left in front of his chest. If this happens, Black will issue force with his left hand, causing Grey's right elbow to collapse. Grey will then be unable to neutralize as he gets pushed back and to his left.

3. Black's right hand slides to the top of Grey's left arm, just above the elbow. At the same time, Grey's right hand arcs down and right, to end touching the outside of Black's left elbow or forearm (see figure 6.3).

Figure 6.3

This is a critical movement. Grey must make sure that his right forearm remains connected to Black throughout its arc to the right. If Grey disconnects or loses continuity at this point, Black may issue force through Black's left hand, and Grey will be unable to neutralize. The reason for this is that Grey has little freedom to turn his waist across the "closed" right hip (refer to section 4.7). Grey will therefore break Black's attack by using his right forearm to press in against Black's left, effectively jamming Black's left elbow.

If Black instead issues force with his right hand, Grey neutralizes by turning his waist slightly left and rotating the left elbow down.

4. Grey begins to shift his weight forward as his left hand (sliding to connect at Black's wrist) pushes Black's left hand up and away toward the right side of Black's chest. At the same time,

Grey's right hand begins to roll over the top of Black's left elbow. Black neutralizes by bending his left elbow and beginning to shift his weight back. At the same time, Black's right hand moves to the inside of Black's left elbow (see figure 6.4).

*Figure 6.4*

*Figure 6.5*

This hand position is the mirror image of figure 6.1. As Grey's right hand rolls over Black's left elbow, Black must be careful that his elbow does not cross in toward his chest. If this happens, Grey can trap Black's elbow and push him out.

5. Grey's left hand continues down toward the right side of Black's chest, as Grey's right hand rolls over the top of Black's left elbow and onto Black's right hand. At the same time, Grey completes his forward weight shift as Black completes his backward weight shift. Black's left hand follows Grey's left hand, arcing down to Black's right elbow (see figure 6.5).

This hand position is the mirror image of figure 6.2. As in the previous step, Black must remain alert to ensure that his left elbow does not cross in front of his chest.

6. Grey's left hand slides to the top of Black's right arm, just above the elbow. At the same time, Black's left hand arcs down and left, to end touching the outside of Grey's right elbow or forearm (see figure 6.6).

*Figure 6.6*

This hand position is a mirror image of figure 6.3. Black must make sure that his left forearm remains connected to Grey throughout its arc to the left. If Black disconnects or loses continuity, Grey may issue force through Grey's right hand, causing Black's unsupported right hand to collapse in toward his chest. Although Black has freedom to turn his waist to the left (unlike the mirrored posture in step (3), where Grey is working across his own closed hip), Black will have difficulty returning the force back to Grey without the support of Black's left arm.

If Grey issues force with his left hand, Black neutralizes by rotating his right elbow down and pressing in on Grey's right arm (thus diverting Grey's advancing energy to Grey's left).

7. Black begins to shift his weight forward as his right hand (sliding to connect at Grey's wrist) pushes Grey's right hand up and away toward the left side of Grey's chest. At the same time, Black's left hand begins to roll over the top of Grey's right elbow. Grey neutralizes by bending his right elbow and beginning to

shift his weight back. At the same time, Grey's left hand moves to the inside of Grey's left elbow (see figure 6.7).

Figure 6.7

This position is the same as figure 6.1. As Black's left hand rolls over Grey's right elbow, Grey must be careful that his elbow does not cross in toward his chest. If this happens, Black can trap Grey's elbow and push him out.

At the end of step (7), steps (2) through (7) are repeated as many times as desired. After an interval of practice in this way, the direction of the hand movements may be reversed so that Grey performs Black's movements and vice versa. Also, the stance may be changed to the opposite foot with a step in either direction: one partner initiates a step forward or backward, and the other follows. The hand movements should continue without break while the step takes place.

A vital feature of this exercise is correct interpretation of the relative force being applied by each of the opponent's two hands. Even if the opponent intends to advance with equal force on both sides, the distribution is never exactly symmetrical. The neutralizing party must be highly sensitive to this disparity and use the energy of the heavier side against the lighter one. To train this sensitivity *(ting jin* and *dong jin)*, it is necessary to practice slowly and deliberately.

The student should pay particular attention to neutralization across the closed hip. This is the most difficult spot in the sequence. In particular, be certain that your waist never turns to full extension on the closed side. If this happens, you can become instantly jammed. It is a good idea to have your partner "feed" you by repeatedly pressing slowly and steadily on your closed side until you can return the force without tensing.

Above all, do not get discouraged. This ostensibly simple exercise takes at least two years to learn properly, and several more to do reasonably well.

## Moving Step

Moving-step *(da lü)* push-hands is the essential combat exercise of Chen Style Taijiquan. It is a highly dynamic exercise in the sense that the action of the opponents can change completely as a result of minor shifts in emphasis or tactical approach. For example, a slight backward press instead of a forward press in step (7) can lead to an entirely different set of dynamics, in spite of the fact that the externally visible movements remain the same. Presented below is the most basic form of the exercise. Students may find their own variations as their skill increases (in Taiji, skill imparts freedom).

Note that the hand movements (except for the grasping and pulling part) are the same as in the previous exercise, but the direction reverses with each step.

1. Grey and Black face each other at a slightly wider distance than in the fixed-step exercise from the previous section. Grey sinks and steps toward Black at a twenty-five-degree angle with his left foot. At the same time, Grey raises both hands in front of his chest. Black steps to the inside of Grey's left foot with his right foot so that their knees touch. Black raises his right forearm so that the wrist connects with Grey's right wrist and the elbow connects with Grey's left hand. Black places his left hand

*Figure 6.8*                                      *Figure 6.9*

on the inside of his right elbow. Black's weight is slightly forward, and Grey's weight is slightly back (see figure 6.8).

2. Black's right hand arcs down past his left elbow. Grey's right
   hand follows and slides onto Black's left elbow (see figure 6.9).

3. Black's right hand continues its arc down and right, then comes
   up outside of Grey's left elbow (see figure 6.10).

4. Grey's left hand arcs up and right as Grey's right hand moves
   to the inside of his left elbow. At the same time, Grey's weight
   shifts slightly forward, and Black's weight shifts slightly back.
   Black's left hand follows Grey's left hand, while Black's right
   hand rolls over the top of Grey's left elbow (see figure 6.11).

*Figure 6.10*                                     *Figure 6.11*

This hand position is the mirror image of figure 6.8.

5. Grey's left hand arcs down past his right elbow. Black's left hand follows and slides onto Grey's right elbow (see figure 6.12).

This hand position is the mirror image of figure 6.9.

6. Grey's left hand continues its arc down and left, then lifts up high under Black's upper right arm. At the same time, Grey's right hand rolls over the top of Black's right hand and *lightly* grasps Black's fingers across the proximal phalanx bones (the finger bones closest to the palm). The main grip is achieved with closing pressure between Grey's thumb and third finger; Grey's index finger rests slightly higher up on the back of Black's hand and provides extra control. While Grey lifts with his left hand and grasps with his right, Black's left hand moves toward the inside of Black's right elbow (see figure 6.13).

It is a serious tactical error to grab any part of the opponent unless the action allows you to control the opponent *immediately*. For this reason, Grey's grasp on Black's right hand must be light. If Grey's gentle lifting of Black's right arm induces Black to resist and push down, then Grey will sense it; he may then use his grasp to apply a technique.

*Figure 6.12*

*Figure 6.13*

7. Black's right hand presses in toward the left side of Grey's chest. Grey neutralizes Black's press by sinking back on his right leg and pulling Black's right arm past Grey's body. As Grey pulls (lightly), Black follows, sinking into his right leg, and pressing directly toward Grey's center with his right upper arm and shoulder. Grey redirects Black's press outward using his hands and waist and threatens to lock Black's right elbow

Figure 6.14

by pressing down with his left wrist. Black protects his right elbow with his left hand (see figure 6.14).

Throughout this exercise, but particularly in this movement, the legs play both an offensive and defensive role. If Black senses through his right knee that Grey is not solidly rooted, he may use his knee and upper body to unbalance Grey backward. If Grey similarly senses that Black is unrooted, he may drive Black's right knee forward (but, since this is friendly practice, not into the ground) while locking Black's right elbow.

8. Black neutralizes Grey's threatened elbow-press by relaxing his right shoulder and sinking his right elbow down. Black then follows through with his right hand, lifting it up and back and threatening to press Grey backward. At the same time, Black rises up and begins to shift his weight back to his left leg. Grey follows Black's lifting motion with both of his hands, also rising and shifting his weight forward onto his left leg. As Grey moves

forward, Black's left hand moves to Grey's right elbow to prevent Grey from entering with an elbow strike. Grey's left hand serves the same function at Black's right elbow (see figure 6.15).

9. As Grey continues to press toward Black, Black yields by stepping backward with his right foot (observing proper stepping procedure, as discussed in Chapter 4). Grey follows, stepping forward and placing his right foot inside Black's left foot so that the knees touch. When Black's right elbow is no longer a threat, Grey's left hand moves to the inside of Grey's right elbow. Grey then continues to press forward with his upper right arm and shoulder, shifting his weight to the right foot as Black yields by shifting weight back to his left foot (see figure 6.16).

*Figure 6.15*

*Figure 6.16*

At this point, Grey and Black repeat steps (2) through (9) with the roles reversed (see figures 6.17 through 6.24; figure 6.24 reprises the starting position from step (1)) and continue through as many iterations as desired. After an interval of practice in this way, the exercise should be practiced on the opposite side. To make the transition, either of the partners simply steps *behind* (rather than inside)

Figure 6.17

Figure 6.18

Figure 6.19

Figure 6.20

the other's foot when it is his turn to advance. Action then continues with step (5) (instead of step (2)), but with left and right directions reversed. For example, Grey would change sides by stepping behind Black's left foot in step (9). Since Grey is again on the pulling side (the party whose foot is behind always does the pulling), he omits one circuit of the hands by going directly to step (5) and pulls Black down to the left instead of the right. Steps (2) through (9) are then repeated normally, but with left and right directions reversed.

One of the most difficult aspects of this extremely difficult exercise is the leg technique. Both parties have approximately equal advantage when their stances meet at an angle of about 125 to 135

Figure 6.21

Figure 6.22

Figure 6.23

Figure 6.24

degrees. If the angle is more acute, the opponent with the inside position has an advantage; if it is more obtuse, the outside opponent has an advantage. Also, the opponent with the outside position should have the toe of his leading foot turned in somewhat. This enables better offensive use of the knee (and is the reason for the foot-turning techniques described in section 4.7 and used in movements such as Angled Body Fist). The inside opponent should have the toe of his leading foot less turned in than his counterpart. In general, the feet are free to turn as needed. The back foot is also free to shift its position if either opponent dislikes the angle of his stance relative to the other.

Large moving-step push-hands (*da peng/da lü*) is similar to normal moving-step push-hands, except that it is practiced with lower stances and an extra repetition of the pulling movement. After step (7), Grey shifts his weight forward, pressing toward Black with his left upper arm and shoulder, while Grey's left hand arcs up and right and his right hand moves to the inside of his left elbow. Black shifts his weight back in response while his left hand connects with Grey's left hand at the wrist, and his right hand moves to Grey's left elbow. This position is now the same as the one in figure 6.11. Action continues at step (5), and the sequence repeats as usual. Throughout the entire exercise, both participants should stay as low as in figure 6.14. This requires considerable leg conditioning, which is why the exercise is only practiced at advanced levels of training.

# ✠ 6.2 Push-Hands Applications

There is nothing special about Taiji's combat applications; in fact, many Taiji applications have similar counterparts in other martial arts such as Shaolin and Jujitsu. There are only so many ways to lock a joint or strike with an elbow, so it is not surprising that the methods for accomplishing these things are frequently reinvented. Those of my students who are adept in other martial arts are often surprised when I allow them (at the appropriate point in their development) to use any *correct* technique of their choosing—whether or not it is a "Taiji" technique. There are, of course, many *in*correct techniques, namely those that employ incorrect body mechanics. When the student has reached the level where she is training in free-form applications, however, she should know the difference between the two without having to analyze. Moreover, even many incorrect techniques can be adapted for use with correct body mechanics.

When facing an opponent, it is essential to avoid harboring any preconceptions about how the engagement will evolve; in other words, it is a mistake to fixate on techniques. Your focus should be on interpreting the opponent's force and structure. One of my teachers puts it this way: "When you drip water on a dog's back, the dog shakes instantly, without considering how, and before he is even aware of doing it. This is how you must respond to the opponent."

When the opponent advances, you will draw out his force up to the point where he is exerting maximum effort (this usually occurs at nearly full extension along whichever vector the attack propagates), then issue. Your counterattack will proceed along a vector that does not directly oppose the other's force. This may mean that you yield to his force directly and cause him to overextend in the same direction that he is already going, but more often, it means that you either redirect or issue force at an angle. The important thing to note is that your counterattack occurs *while you are neutralizing,* not after. In Taiji, there is no latency between defense and attack. In fact, there is no *difference* between defense and attack except in the amount of energy returned to the opponent. Li Yi Yu, perhaps the most insightful author ever on the subject of Taijiquan combat, writes:

> When your training has reached the level of emptiness,
> The distinction of offense and defense no longer exists.

It is permissible to initiate an attack "from scratch" if you are sufficiently sure of the target (in particular, that it will still be there when your attack arrives). The best way to do this is to strike at precisely the instant when the opponent is about to issue force or initiate a change. This method is called "striking the contained energy" and obviously requires high skill in *dong jin*. An easier approach is to initiate a small advance (a feint, essentially) that induces the opponent to react or forces him to take action in order to avoid a tactical loss. You then neutralize the reaction and counterattack in the usual way.

Whether initiating or responding, your objective is the same: attack at the moment when the opponent has exhausted his freedom. An opponent without freedom cannot neutralize. An opponent on the point of attacking or initiating a change has no freedom because his intention is committed to his planned action (which is why striking contained energy is effective). What about the case of a careful advance (that is, an advance into your territory that does not occur as an outright attack)? If you simply yield to the advance and allow the opponent to occupy your space, and if the opponent is skilled enough not to overextend or become unbalanced, then your own freedom diminishes because of the sacrificed space. You may retreat, but any such forced action also sacrifices freedom. Yielding, by itself, is therefore ineffective. The *Yang Family Forty Chapters* summarizes this problem:

> What is difficult is holding to the central earth.
> Retreat is easy but advance most difficult.

A world of meaning is encompassed by these two lines, but, as with most of the material in the Taijiquan "classics," it is incomprehensible except to those who already understand it.

Stated simply, the main tactical challenge of Taijiquan combat is this: how do you yield (in other words, not resist) without retreating or sacrificing space ("central earth")? The answer is that yielding never happens by itself. Any advance introduces a change in the overall dynamic of the engagement, and your job is to find points in your opponent's structure that have emptied out as a result of the change. You will then flow into these points, occupying the opponent's space and diminishing his freedom, even while you yield to his advance. Your opponent should lose space (and, consequently, freedom) every time he moves.

For example, if you stand in a left-weighted, front bow-stance and your opponent pushes your right shoulder, one way to neutralize his advance is to allow your right shoulder to rotate back while your left side rotates forward, consuming his space. This is perhaps the easiest case to understand. If the opponent pushes your left (weighted) side, the situation is less simple. Since you have limited freedom to turn in the direction of the closed hip, you must find a vector that will allow you to redirect the force without running out of room. This will often mean that you add force of your own to direct your opponent's force either up or down. At the same time, you will consume his space above, below, or on the opposite side. Note that in doing this, your action neither directly resists nor directly yields to the opponent; you meet him at an angle. Another general case is when the opponent advances on more than one side simultaneously. As explained earlier, you will establish a fulcrum and use the force of the heavier side against the lighter one. In these cases it is often permissible to oppose the lighter force directly because the opponent is essentially acting against himself.

The success or failure of any Taiji technique depends on correct interpretation of the opponent's structure (which, in turn, depends on coherent movement). Anyone who has had the childhood experience of looking in a martial-arts book and trying a few of the tricks out on some friends knows an important fact: techniques (*any* techniques) do not work. It makes no difference how well you learn them. Opponents do not cooperate, and minute variations in set-up or execution can completely change the result. If you only know techniques, then the engagement is simply a contest of strength and speed.

Any advanced Taijiquan instructor should be able to provide the following demonstration: take the instructor's arm (which remains completely relaxed) and try to lock it—bend it, twist the wrist, the hand, whatever you like. Nothing you do allows you to lock the instructor or control her, in spite of the fact that she takes no active counter-measures. Next, give the instructor your arm and observe the difference in the outcome.

By now, you know why this happens. The instructor interprets your energy and neutralizes using adjustments that are too small for you to detect. Conversely, you cannot defend against her lock because she understands your structure better than you yourself. It makes no difference which techniques you use, and it makes no difference which techniques she uses. The opponent with higher skill in interpreting energy is the one who wins.

Applications, therefore, are like a buffet. You may use the morsels that suit your tastes, as long as you already know how to eat.

## ✖ Application #1: **Forward Pull-Down**

1. This technique begins at the transition into step (7) of the moving-step push-hands exercise. In this example, Black is pulling (see figure 6.25).

*Figure 6.25*

2. Black shifts his weight back to his right leg while his right hand lightly pulls Grey down to the right and his left hand controls Grey's right elbow. At the same time, Grey presses into Black with his right arm and shoulder but allows his arm to overextend (see figure 6.26).

3. Black senses Grey's overextension and immediately locks Grey's right elbow by rotating it up (twisting Grey's right hand medially so that the elbow turns up) and issuing force downward against the elbow with his left hand. Once the lock is established and Grey is on the ground, Black increases his control by sliding his left hand behind Grey's right shoulder and continuing to rotate Grey's right arm up. While doing this, Black maintains the lock on Grey's right wrist so that Grey cannot use arm strength to resist (see figure 6.27).

*Figure 6.26*

*Figure 6.27*

## ✖ Application #2: **Backward Press**

1. This technique also begins at the transition into step (7) of the moving-step push-hands exercise. Black is again pulling (see figure 6.28).

*Figure 6.28*

2. Black attempts to use his right hand to pull Grey forward but fails to coordinate the movement with the rest of his body (in other words, he loses connection). Grey redirects Black's pull, using his right shoulder and arm to press directly into Black's center. At this point, Black is completely out of room (see figure 6.29).

3. Grey uses his right arm and shoulder and also his left hand to issue force directly into Black's chest, pushing Black backward and causing him to lose balance (see figure 6.30).

*Figure 6.29*

*Figure 6.30*

## ✖ Application #3: **Forward Shoulder Strike**

1. This technique begins at the transition into step (8) of the moving-step push-hands exercise. Grey has finished pulling and Black is beginning his backward weight shift in preparation to step back with his right foot (see figure 6.31).

2. Black shifts weight to his left leg and begins to step backward with his right foot. Grey begins to step forward but commits his weight too early. Also, he holds on too long to Black's right hand (see figure 6.32).

3. Black senses that Grey is slightly over-balanced in his forward step. Black immediately reverses his direction (he can do this because he was stepping with correct technique), planting his right foot forward behind Grey's right foot. At the same time, Black uses Grey's grip on his right hand (twisting his hand around and gripping Grey's hand himself, in this example) to pull Grey's right arm up and away to Black's right. As soon as Grey's arm is out of the way, Black brings the point of his right

Figure 6.31

Figure 6.32

shoulder sharply forward and issues force into Grey's ribs, directly below Grey's right shoulder. Black's left hand simultaneously issues force against Grey's lower back, as Black's right hip and thigh issue force against Grey's right hip and thigh (see figure 6.33).

4. Grey is knocked back (see figure 6.34).

*Figure 6.33*

*Figure 6.34*

In this example, Grey inadvertently assists Black's attack by failing to let go of Black's right hand. Black exploits Grey's error by using Grey's grip to pull his right arm out of the way, thus exposing Grey's ribs. If Grey does not commit this error, Black may achieve the same objective by briefly grasping Grey's wrist or hand.

This technique is far more dangerous than it first appears. When practicing, it is imperative to place the attacking shoulder gently on its target, then use very light force to push the opponent back. Failure to do so may result in broken ribs.

## ⚔ Application #4: **Inward Wrist Lock**

1. This technique begins at the end of step (4) of the moving-step push-hands exercise. Black's left hand has arced up as his right hand moved to the inside of his left elbow (see figure 6.35). This is the same position as figure 6.19.

*Figure 6.35*

2. Black's left hand arcs down past his right elbow. Grey's left hand follows and slides onto Black's right elbow (see figure 6.36).

3. Black's left hand continues its arc down and left, then lifts up high under Grey's upper right arm. At the same time, Black's right hand rolls over the top of Grey's right hand and lightly grasps Grey's fingers across the proximal phalanx bones. The main grip is achieved with closing pressure between Black's thumb and third finger; Black's index finger rests slightly higher up on the back of Grey's hand and provides extra control (see figure 6.37).

*Figure 6.36*

*Figure 6.37*

4. Grey issues force into Black's left shoulder with Grey's right hand but fails to connect with Black's center. Black neutralizes Grey's press by sinking back slightly onto his right leg and turning his waist left. As Grey's right hand slides off to the side of Black's chest, Black exploits Grey's force by tightening his grip on Grey's hand and pulling it through to Black's left while bending it backward and twisting it in toward Grey. At the same time, Black increases the pressure on Grey's wrist by pressing down on Grey's upper right arm with his left hand (see figure 6.38).

5. With the lock established, Black increases his control by using his left hand to press Grey forward (see figure 6.39).

This lock is fairly difficult to learn. Students should practice slowly, using a combination of three forces against the opponent's hand: backward bending of the opponent's wrist, an inward twist (that is, twisting the opponent's fingers in toward the opponent), and medial rotation (the opponent's hand rotates medially; the attacker's rotates laterally).

Figure 6.38

Figure 6.39

# ⚹ Application #5: **Arm Cross with Knee Jam**

1. This technique begins at step (2) of the moving-step push-hands exercise (see figure 6.40). This position is the same as figure 6.16.

*Figure 6.40*

2. Grey's right hand arcs down past his left elbow. Black's right hand follows Grey's then slides onto Grey's elbow. Grey allows his left elbow to move to the right, crossing slightly in front of his chest. Black senses this and grasps Grey's left hand with his own left (see figure 6.41).

3. Black pulls Grey sharply to Black's left. At the same time, Black's right hand pushes Grey's left elbow left and forward, while Black's left knee presses inward on Grey's right knee. Grey is twisted across his closed hip and falls to his right (see figure 6.42).

*Figure 6.41*

*Figure 6.42*

## ⌘ Application #6: **Wrist Lock with Elbow Trap**

1. This technique begins at the transition into step (8) of the moving-step push-hands exercise. Grey has finished pulling and Black is beginning his backward weight shift in preparation to step back with his right foot (see figure 6.43).

2. Grey releases his grasp on Black's right hand and connects to Black's right wrist. Black shifts his weight to his left leg and begins to step backward with his right foot. As Grey begins to step forward, he loses connection in his right arm. Black detects this and lightly grasps Grey's right hand with his own right (see figure 6.44).

3. Black quickly steps behind Grey's right foot with his own right. At the same time, Black folds Grey's right hand down and in toward Grey's chest, simultaneously trapping Grey's right elbow with Black's left hand. Black continues to apply downward-folding pressure against Grey's right wrist, bracing Grey's right elbow against Black's right upper arm. Black bends Grey backward across Black's right knee, and Grey is immobilized (see figure 6.45).

*Figure 6.43*　　　　*Figure 6.44*　　　　*Figure 6.45*

# ✖ Application #7:
# **Backward Wrist Lock**

1. This technique begins at the transition into step (8) of the moving-step push-hands exercise. Grey has finished pulling and Black is beginning his backward weight shift in preparation to step back with his right foot (see figure 6.46).

2. Black shifts his weight to his left leg and begins to step backward with his right foot. As Grey begins to step forward, he allows his right palm to face forward, toward Black. Black immediately steps forward, placing his right foot inside Grey's right foot. At the same time, Black grasps the palm side of Grey's right hand with his own right and bends Grey's hand backward, simultaneously twisting Grey's hand medially and controlling Grey's right elbow with his left hand (see figure 6.47).

*Figure 6.46*

*Figure 6.47*

## ✖ Application #8: **Lateral Wrist Lock with Arm Wrap**

1. This technique begins at the end of step (5) of the moving-step push-hands exercise. Grey's left hand has just arced down past his right elbow, and Black's right hand has slid to the elbow (see figure 6.48).

2. Grey's left hand continues its travel down, left, and up under Black's right elbow. At the same time, Grey begins to reach for the top of Black's right hand in preparation for the grasp and pull. Black induces Grey to reach slightly farther than usual by allowing his (Black's) right hand to travel to the right and up as his left hand slides up Grey's forearm. As Grey's right hand follows Black's, Grey mistakenly allows his right elbow to cross slightly to his left, in front of his chest. Black immediately grasps the back of Grey's right hand with his own left. Black achieves the grasp by wrapping his third, fourth, and fifth fingers around the base of Grey's thumb and using the tip of his own thumb to press against the end of Grey's fifth metacarpal bone (see figure 6.49).

*Figure 6.48*

*Figure 6.49*

3. Black quickly twists Grey's right hand laterally toward Black's left while slicing his right arm down over the top of Grey's right elbow. (If Grey's elbow had not crossed in front of his chest in the previous step, Black would have had a harder time immobilizing Grey's forearm.) Black establishes the lock by using both twisting and folding pressure against Grey's right wrist (see figure 6.50).

4. Black increases his control by wrapping his right arm around Grey's right arm and sliding his right hand up Grey's chest toward his throat (see figure 6.51).

This lock is another that is very difficult to learn. Students should master the lateral wrist lock by itself (one-handed) before attempting the whole technique.

*Figure 6.50*

*Figure 6.51*

## ✖ Application #9: **Wrist Grab Reversal**

1. Grey and Black face each other squarely. Black steps forward with his right foot and grabs Grey's right wrist (see figure 6.52).

2. Grey steps his left foot forward behind Black's right foot. At the same time, Grey raises his right hand slightly, keeping it close to his body. This induces Black to tighten his grip on Grey's wrist. Grey "helps" Black maintain his grip by placing his left hand firmly over Black's right and using his fingertips to grip the side of Black's index finger (see figure 6.53).

3. Maintaining a firm grip on Black's right hand (particularly the index finger), Grey turns his waist right. At the same time, Grey brings his own right hand up and over the top of Black's right wrist. Both of Grey's hands then press downward in a motion that both scissors and twists. The effect is that Black's right hand is simultaneously twisted medially and bent sideways so that his fifth finger moves toward his forearm. Once the lock is established, Grey may use his left elbow against Black's right elbow to gain further control (see figure 6.54).

*Figure 6.52*

*Figure 6.53*

*Figure 6.54*

## ✕ Application #10: **Two-Handed Backward Wrist Lock**

1. Grey's right hand grasps the palm side of Black's right hand and applies force, attempting to bend it backward (see figure 6.55).

*Figure 6.55*

2. Black yields to Grey's force by quickly pulling his right hand back and to Black's right. When Grey reacts and tries to retrieve his hand, Black (remaining connected to Grey's structure even through this very rapid movement) again follows his force, folding Grey's wrist back toward Grey. With the lock established, Black steps forward with his left foot and brings his left forearm up under Grey's armpit (see figure 6.56).

3. Maintaining his lock on Grey's wrist, Black winds his left hand over the top of Grey's right forearm then presses the edge of his hand straight down against Grey's wrist. Grey is immobilized (see figure 6.57).

*Figure 6.56*

*Figure 6.57*

## ⌖ Application #11: **Backward Arm Split**

Figure 6.58

1. This technique begins at step (5) of the moving-step push-hands exercise. Black's left hand is arcing down past her right elbow (see figure 6.58).

2. Black's left hand continues up behind Grey's right upper arm as Black lightly grasps Grey's right hand with her own right. Grey begins to press in with her right hand against the left side of Black's chest (see figure 6.59).

3. Grey's press is premature. Black neutralizes by turning her waist slightly left and quickly brings her left hand down, then up inside Grey's right elbow. Black maintains a firm grasp on Grey's right hand or wrist while using her left forearm to issue force to Black's left. At the same time, Black presses forward against Grey's right knee with her left knee. Grey is thrown backward (see figure 6.60).

Figure 6.59

Figure 6.60

# ✖ Application #12: **Head Twist**

1. This technique begins at step (5) of the moving-step push-hands exercise. Black's left hand is arcing down past her right elbow (see figure 6.61).

*Figure 6.61*

2. Black's left hand continues up behind Grey's right upper arm as Black lightly grasps Grey's right hand with her own right. As in the previous application, Grey begins to press in with her right hand against the left side of Black's chest (see figure 6.62).

3. Black neutralizes by turning her waist right and using her right hand to redirect Grey's press forward and to Black's right. Black does not shift her weight while doing this. Instead, she allows Grey to draw closer then uses her left hand to reach around the back of Grey's head and grasp her chin. She then twists Grey's head to Grey's left and presses against Grey's right knee with her (Black's) left knee. At the same time, she continues to pull on Grey's right arm. Grey is immobilized (see figure 6.63).

*Figure 6.62*

*Figure 6.63*

# ✠ Application #13: **Throat Lock**

*Figure 6.64*

1. This technique begins at step (9) of the moving-step push-hands exercise. Grey has just stepped forward, and her right hand is beginning its arc down toward her left elbow (see figure 6.64).

2. As Grey's right hand continues down toward her left elbow, she anticipates Black's downward push and loses connection with Black's right hand. Black feels the break and immediately slides her right hand up to Grey's throat as Black's left hand moves off Grey's right elbow and goes to the base of Grey's back (see figure 6.65).

3. Black uses her left hand to press forward against Grey's lower back while using her right hand against Grey's throat to press Grey backward (see figure 6.66).

*Figure 6.65*

*Figure 6.66*

# Appendix

## Catalog of Forms

The task of translating Taiji forms is extraordinarily difficult. Many of the movement names are so metaphorical (or metonymical) that they lose meaning altogether when rendered literally into English. For example, movement (43) of the Second Form is literally "Turn Head Block Straight Enter Well" *(hui tou jing lan zhi ru)*. The movement in question is a 360-degree turn, followed by a short, direct issue of force. The expression "enter well" therefore refers metaphorically to a very direct action (a well goes straight down). I translate this movement as "Turn Around, Short Issue." Movement (21) of the glaive form is literally "Next lift green dragon see dead people" *(zai ju qing long kan si ren)*. The "green dragon" in this case is the glaive, and the "dead people" are actually enemies who are *about* to be dead. Thus, the translation is "Raise glaive, survey the doomed." In other cases, a "green dragon" is really just a green dragon, as in movement (17) in the First Form.

Even literal descriptions pose certain ambiguities. Movement (33) of the "Five Tigers Swarming Sheep" Staff form is called *gong bu dian gun*. The word *dian* in this case means "point"; however, in the next movement, *cha bu dian gun*, the word *dian* means "tap." The only way to know this is to know the movement.

The forms are replete with translational problems such as these. Because accuracy requires an intimate knowledge of the movements themselves, other printed translations are likely to differ somewhat from those that follow.

# First Form *(Di Yi Lu)*

1. Opening Movement
2. Diamond King Pounds Mortar
3. Lazily Tucking Clothes
4. Six Sealing, Four Closing
5. Single Whip
6. Diamond King Pounds Mortar
7. White Goose Spreads Wings
8. Oblique Posture
9. Embrace Knee
10. Twist Steps
11. Oblique Posture
12. Embrace Knee
13. Twist Steps
14. Covered Hand Punch
15. Diamond King Pounds Mortar
16. Angled Body Fist
17. Green Dragon Emerges from Water
18. Two-Handed Push
19. Fist Under Elbow
20. Step Back and Swing Arms
21. White Goose Spreads Wings
22. Oblique Posture
23. Flash the Back
24. Covered Hand Punch

25. Six Sealing, Four Closing

26. Single Whip

27. Hand Technique

28. High Pat on Horse

29. Slap Right Foot

30. Slap Left Foot

31. Left Heel Kick

32. Advance Carefully with Twist Steps

33. Grasp and Hit

34. Double Kick

35. Protect the Heart Punch

36. Tornado Kick

37. Right Heel Kick

38. Covered Hand Punch

39. Small Catch and Hit

40. Embrace Head, Push Mountain

41. Six Sealing, Four Closing

42. Single Whip

43. Forward Technique

44. Backward Technique

45. Part the Mustang's Mane

46. Six Sealing, Four Closing

47. Single Whip

48. Jade Maiden Works Shuttles

49. Lazily Tucking Clothes

50. Six Sealing, Four Closing

51. Single Whip

52. Hand Technique

53. Swing Foot

54. Drop and Split
55. Golden Rooster Stands on One Leg
56. Step Back and Swing Arms
57. White Goose Spreads Wings
58. Oblique Posture
59. Flash the Back
60. Covered Hand Punch
61. Six Sealing, Four Closing
62. Single Whip
63. Hand Technique
64. High Pat on Horse
65. Cross Foot
66. Groin Punch
67. Monkey Picks Fruit
68. Single Whip
69. Dragon Hacks the Ground
70. Step Up, Make Seven Stars
71. Step Back, Open Arms
72. Sweep Foot
73. Head-on Cannon
74. Diamond King Pounds Mortar
75. Closing Movement

## Second Form *(Di Er Lu)*

The Second Form is also called Cannon Bashing *(pao chui)*. Some modern practitioners of this form add a Diamond King Pounds Mortar movement at the end in order to preserve the same symmetry found in the First Form. The original version does not include this movement.

1. Opening Movement
2. Diamond King Pounds Mortar
3. Lazily Tucking Clothes
4. Six Sealing, Four Closing
5. Single Whip
6. Protect the Heart Punch
7. Oblique Posture
8. Turn Around, Diamond King Pounds Mortar
9. Angled Body Fist
10. Groin Strike
11. Chop Hand
12. Overturn Flower
13. Flick Sleeves
14. Covered Hand Punch
15. Elbow Intercepts at Waist
16. Big Arm Technique
17. Small Arm Technique
18. Jade Maiden Works Shuttles
19. Turn and Ride the Dragon
20. Covered Hand Punch
21. Wrapped Firecracker
22. Beast Head Posture
23. Expansive Pose
24. Covered Hand Punch
25. Tame the Tiger
26. Wipe Brow
27. Yellow Dragon Stirs Water Three Times
28. Left Rush
29. Right Rush

30. Covered Hand Punch
31. Sweep the Hall
32. Covered Hand Punch
33. All Cannons Pound
34. Covered Hand Punch
35. Strike Groin, Strike Heart
36. Left Head-Level Strike
37. Right Head-Level Strike
38. Turn Around, Head-on Cannon
39. Change Position, Large Cannon
40. Elbow Intercepts at Waist
41. Pursue with Elbow
42. Deep Cannon
43. Turn Around, Short Issue
44. Closing Movement

## Sphere *(Taiji Qiu)*

1.  Draw Up Ball
2.  Na Jia Explores Sea (Left)
3.  Na Jia Explores Sea (Right)
4.  Cover Moon (Left)
5.  Cover Moon (Right)
6.  Tyrant Raises Censer
7.  Wei Tuo Offers Staff
8.  Lion Rolls Ball
9.  Lure Spider into Cave
10. Support Thousand Pounds (Left)
11. Pearl Returns to Nest
12. Wei Tuo Offers Staff

13. Lion Rolls Ball

14. Lure Spider into Cave

15. Support Thousand Pounds (Right)

16. Pearl Returns to Nest

17. Fiery Spider Tempts Dragon

18. Closing Movement

## Straight Sword (Dan Jian)

1.  Opening Movement

2.  Face the Sun

3.  Immortal Points the Way

4.  Green Dragon Emerges from Water

5.  Protect the Knees

6.  Close the Door

7.  Green Dragon Emerges from Water

8.  Turn and Chop

9.  Green Dragon Turns Body

10. Diagonal Flying Posture

11. Spread Wings

12. Bow Head

13. Fan Grass to Search for Snake

14. Golden Rooster Stands on One Leg

15. Immortal Points the Way

16. Sink and Block with Stomp

17. Ancient Tree Wraps Roots

18. Hungry Tiger Pounces on Food

19. Green Dragon Swings Tail

20. Step Back and Swing Sword

21. Mustang Jumps Creek

22. White Snake Flicks Tongue
23. Black Dragon Swings Tail
24. Zhong Kui Brandishes Sword
25. Luohan Subdues Dragon
26. Black Bear Turns Back
27. Swallow Pecks Dirt
28. White Snake Flicks Tongue
29. Diagonal Flying Posture
30. Eagle and Bear Match Wits
31. Swallow Pecks Dirt
32. Pluck Stars, Transform to Dipper
33. Scoop Moon from Sea Bottom
34. Phoenix Nods Head
35. Swallow Pecks Dirt
36. White Snake Flicks Tongue
37. Diagonal Flying Posture
38. Support Thousand Pounds (Left)
39. Support Thousand Pounds (Right)
40. Swallow Pecks Dirt
41. White Ape Presents Fruit
42. Falling Flowers Movement
43. Up, Down Diagonal Thrust
44. Diagonal Flying Posture
45. Na Jia Explores the Sea
46. Exotic Python Turns Body
47. Wei Tuo Presents Staff
48. Grind the Basin
49. Return to Origin

# Double Straight-Sword *(Shuang Jian)*

The double straight-sword is primarily a demonstration form, and a recent addition to the system. According to Chen Qing Zhou, it was developed by Chen Zhao Pei in the early twentieth century.

1. Falling Flowers, Flowing Water, Face the Sun
2. Beautiful Girl Turns to Watch Moon
3. Ye Cha Explores the Sea
4. Black Bear Turns Back, Face the Sun
5. Phoenix Turns and Spreads Both Wings
6. Three Thrusts from Above
7. Ancient Tree Wraps Roots
8. Moon Links Three Rings
9. Black Bear Turns Back, Face the Sun
10. Luohan Subdues Dragon (Left)
11. Luohan Subdues Dragon (Right)
12. Turn, Butterfly Draws Water
13. Black Bear Turns Back, Face the Sun
14. Luohan Subdues Dragon (Left)
15. Turn, Er Lang Pushes Mountain
16. Black Bear Turns Back, Face the Sun
17. Zhong Kui Brandishes Sword
18. Ancient Tree Wraps Roots
19. Turn and Chop
20. Black Bear Turns Body, Face the Sun
21. Turn Left and Chop Low
22. Turn Right and Chop Low
23. Turn and Face the Sun
24. Turn and Grind Basin
25. Tyrant Raises Censer

26. Protect the Knees
27. White Snake Flicks Tongue
28. Phoenix Spreads Wings (Left)
29. Phoenix Spreads Wings (Right)
30. Turn and Face the Sun
31. Link Rings, Control Tiger
32. Swords Dance Left and Right
33. Dragon Coils Left
34. Tiger Crouches Right
35. Lion Rolls Silk Ball
36. Part Cloud to Watch Moon
37. Embrace Moon to Chest

## Saber *(Dan Dao)*

Uninformed martial artists, maddeningly, insist on calling the Chinese single-edged sword a "broadsword." This is completely wrong for two reasons:

- A broadsword is a sword with a broad, straight edge. In fact, it usually has two edges and a basket hilt. It bears more resemblance to the Chinese straight sword *(jian)* than to the saber *(dao)*, but really has little relation to either.

- The real Chinese saber is not even "broad." The authentic version of this weapon (contrary to what you see in movies) looks very much like a European saber. It has a narrow, moderately curved blade. The familiar, wide, deeply curved "ox tail" blade was used only briefly by civilians during the nineteenth and early twentieth centuries, and was never used in the Chinese military. This is not the blade for which the Taiji saber form was designed, and in any case, it is a falchion, not a broadsword.

1. Opening Movement
2. Protect the Heart
3. Green Dragon Emerges from Water
4. Wind Rolls Wildflowers
5. White Cloud Covers Head
6. Part Clouds to Gaze at Sun
7. Black Tiger Searches Mountain
8. Su Qin Carries Saber on Back
9. Tumble from Wind
10. Chop White Snake at Waist
11. Sun Links Three Rings
12. Protect the Heart
13. Fan Grass to Search for Snake (Left)
14. Fan Grass to Search for Snake (Right)
15. Green Dragon Emerges from Water
16. Wind Rolls Wildflowers
17. Bird Departs on Golden Wings
18. Ye Cha Explores the Sea
19. Turn Over and Chop (Left)
20. Turn Over and Chop (Right)
21. White Snake Flicks Tongue
22. Embrace Moon to Chest

## Double Saber *(Shuang Dao)*

1. Full Martial Flower, Face the Sun
2. Three Cuts, Face the Sun

3. Cut and Jump
4. Forward, Three Cuts
5. Swallow Departs on Golden Wings
6. Wild Goose Parts from Flock
7. One Cut, Face the Sun
8. Insert Flower (Left)
9. Insert Flower (Right)
10. Two Cuts, Face the Sun
11. Two Cuts, Butterfly Draws Water
12. One Cut, Face the Sun
13. Insert Flower (Left)
14. Insert Flower (Right)
15. Two Cuts, Face the Sun
16. Two Cuts, Subdue the Tiger
17. One Cut, Face the Sun
18. Zhong Kui Brandishes Sword
19. Ancient Tree Wraps Roots
20. Overturn Flower Cut
21. One Cut, Face the Sun
22. Stir Left and Right
23. Two Cuts, Face the Sun
24. Two Cuts, Change Direction
25. Tyrant Raises Censer
26. Luohan Subdues Dragon
27. Protect the Knee
28. Cut Horse Left and Right
29. Two Cuts, Face the Sun
30. White Snake Flicks Tongue
31. Commit to Left and Right

32. Step Up, Make Seven Stars

33. Step Back, Spread Arms

34. Downward Cut

35. Closing Movement

# "Five Tigers Swarming Sheep" Staff
# (Wu Hu Qun Yang Gun)

1.  Opening Movement

2.  Empty Step, Push Palm

3.  Empty Step, Tap Staff

4.  Reverse Lift

5.  Insert Step, Martial Flower (1)

6.  Insert Step, Martial Flower (2)

7.  Reverse Insert Step, Martial Flower

8.  Bow Stance, Press Staff

9.  Reverse Step, Back Staff

10. Right Bow-Stance, Embrace Staff Under Arm

11. Jump and Swat Down

12. Jump and Kick

13. Swing and Chop (Left)

14. Swing and Chop (Right)

15. Swing and Chop (Left)

16. Step Up, Martial Flower, Diagonal Flying Kick

17. Balance and Gaze at Moon

18. Front Leg Sweep

19. Tornado Kick

20. Shake Foot, Left Bow-Stance, Carry Staff on Back

21. Lift Knee, Embrace Staff

22. Side Vault over Staff
23. Martial Flower, Reverse Step, Carry Staff on Back
24. Bow Stance, Press Staff
25. Insert Leg and Balance
26. Tap Staff Left and Right
27. Reverse Step, Carry Staff on Back
28. Throw from Behind, Catch with Opposite Hand
29. Reverse Step, Flip Hand, and Chop
30. Swing, Reverse Step, Carry Staff on Back
31. Left, Right Tap Staff
32. Swing, Strike, Turn, Bow Stance, Tap Staff
33. Bow Stance, Point Staff
34. Insert Step, Tap Staff
35. Swing, Strike, Turn, Bow Stance, Tap Staff
36. Engage the Throat
37. Balance and Gaze at Moon
38. Pump Steps, Carry Staff on Back
39. Close Foot
40. Double Heel Kick to Sky
41. Empty Stance, Tap Staff
42. Throw from Behind
43. Double Kick Staff
44. Empty Stance, Staff Lifts Back to Slap Palm
45. Closing Movement

# Pear Blossom Spear/White Ape Staff (Li Hua Qiang Jia Bai Yuan Gun)

1. Ye Cha Explores the Sea

2.  Full Martial Flower
3.  Mid-Level Thrust
4.  Three Quick Thrusts
5.  Upper-Level Thrust
6.  Swing Pearl-Beaded Curtain
7.  Lower-Level Thrust
8.  Stamp and Thrust
9.  Green Dragon Presents Claws
10. Step Forward, Pierce with Spear
11. Sweep Ground, Block Stab from Side
12. Forward, Two Strikes
13. Yellow Dragon Points Staff
14. Divert Pierce
15. Half Martial Flower
16. Block Attacks at Waist
17. Turn Around, Half Martial Flower
18. Press Down Snake
19. Flick Spear
20. Pierce with Spear
21. Two Finishing Thrusts
22. Wave Banner Left
23. Point to Sky
24. Wave Banner Right
25. Iron Ox Plows Earth
26. Turn Around, Half Martial Flower
27. Water-Dripping Spear
28. Two Finishing Thrusts
29. Step Forward, Ride the Dragon
30. Part Grass to Look for Snake

31. Step Back, White Ape Drags Spear
32. Turn Around, Pin Black Dragon into Cave
33. Stamp and Snatch Pipa
34. Forward, Two Strikes
35. Wield Banner to Sweep Ground
36. Mount Tai Crushes Egg
37. Turn Around, Half Martial Flower
38. Agile Cat Pounces on Mouse
39. Strike from Left
40. Strike from Right
41. Turn and Thrust
42. Flick Heel
43. Single-Handed Thrust
44. Full Martial Flower
45. Er Lang Carries the Mountain
46. Sweep Spear
47. Half Martial Flower
48. Lower Sixty Percent Thrust
49. Turn Around, Half Martial Flower
50. Sparrow Hawk Swoops on Quail
51. Sweep Right
52. Flick Heel
53. Finishing Thrust
54. Full Martial Flower
55. Er Lang Carries the Mountain
56. Sweep Spear
57. Half Martial Flower
58. Beautiful Maiden Holds Needle
59. Jade Maiden Works Shuttles

60. Thrust to Throat

61. Turn and Sweep

62. Full Martial Flower

63. Protect the Knee

64. Two Finishing Thrusts

65. Old Dragon Sweeps Tail

66. Forward Block

67. Forward Block Again

68. Block Left

69. Block Right

70. Half Martial Flower

71. Tai Gong Goes Fishing

72. Step Forward, Mount Horse, Thrust Back

# Three-Opponent Staff
## (San Ren Gan Dui Da)

The three-opponent staff is, as the name implies, a form for three people. The choreography of the form has two participants fighting against one.

1. Opening Movement

2. White Cloud Covers Head

3. Set Formation with Taiji Principles

4. Chop Mountain to Open Road

5. Turn to Break Pressure

6. Carefully Look Right and Left

7. Green Dragonfly Plays in Water

8. Butterfly Chases Dragonfly

9. Sweep Hall and Leap

10. Zhang Fei Beats Drum
11. Hungry Tiger Pounces on Food
12. Sweep Hall and Leap
13. Lou Xin Sweeps North
14. Na Jia Explores Sea
15. Green Dragonfly Plays in Water
16. Butterfly Chases Dragonfly
17. Break Formation, Lose North
18. Return to Origin

## Spring/Autumn Waning Moon Glaive (Chun Qiu Yan Yue Dao)

The list of posture names in the glaive form actually comprises a poem. For this reason, the names are more verbose than names in the other forms.

1. General Guan carries his glaive to Ba Bridge
2. White clouds cover your head, pose like a hero
3. Raise blade as if waving a banner and embracing the moon
4. Three fierce steps forward to frighten Xu Chu
5. Three steps back to frighten Cao Cao
6. White ape drags glaive and cuts upward
7. Full martial flower
8. Angry tiger pounces
9. Who can block the mane-parting blade?
10. Crossed glaive cuts chest
11. Waist-level blade grinds around coiled roots
12. Martial flower releases an upward cut
13. Raise blade as if waving a banner and embracing the moon

14. Martial flower, turn, go right, chop down

15. Blade falls into chest as you embrace the moon

16. Full martial flower, plant the glaive, vault, and cut

17. Backward thrust to intimidate

18. Martial flower, move left, settle into posture

19. Move right, white clouds overhead

20. Martial flower, turn, go left, cut up

21. Raise glaive and survey the doomed

22. Martial flower, move right, settle into posture

23. Move right, white clouds overhead

24. Martial flower, receive wine, pick up cape

25. Martial flower to chop the rod of judgment

26. Who can stop the martial flower with two kicks?

27. Martial flower, bar the gate

28. Waving the curtain, stepping back, the enemy cannot find an opportunity

29. Pose with a raised blade

30. Turn and raise glaive to test the water

# Notes

To avoid confusion, all transliterated words in quoted excerpts have been modified to standard *pinyin* spelling.

## Chapter 1: **Introduction to Taijiquan**

1. The concepts of *taiji* and *wuji* are somewhat more nuanced than I suggest here, and have evolved over time. Zhou Dun Yi (1017–1073) was perhaps the first to differentiate *taiji* from *wuji* in motive terms: *taiji* moves and *wuji* is static. These interpretations are of most practical value to Taijiquan practitioners.

## Chapter 2: **The Evolution of Taijiquan**

1. Huang Zong Xi was a respected scholar who lived during the late Ming and early Qing dynasties. Huang's son, Huang Bai Jia, was the martial-arts student Wang Zheng Nan.
2. Douglas Wile, *Lost T'ai-chi Classics*, p. 26.
3. Wu Yu Xiang was founder of the Small Wu Style of Taijiquan. Li was his nephew and student.
4. Wang Zong Yue's "Treatise on Taijiquan" ("*Taijiquan Lun*") served as the basis for the Taijiquan classics of the Wu and Li families. No one except the Wu brothers ever saw the manuscript, and there is no documented evidence of Wang's actual existence. The story of Yu Xiang obtaining the manuscript in Wu Yang is also rather suspect. It is unlikely that he would have left his widowed mother alone in Guang Ping and travelled to Wu Yang at the outbreak of the Nian Rebellion.
5. Wile, *Lost T'ai-chi Classics*, p. 110.
6. Most of the Taijiquan classics, including important works attributed to the Yang family, were actually written by the Wus.

7. See, for example, Waysun Liao, *T'ai Chi Classics;* Benjamin Lo et al., *The Essence of T'ai Chi Ch'uan;* and Jou Tsung Hwa, *The Tao of Tai-chi Chuan.*

8. In the 1930s, historian Tang Hao found a manuscript in a Beijing bookstall consisting of a "Yin Fu Spear Manual," a "Taijiquan Manual," and a "Spring-Autumn Glaive Manual." The preface to the "Spear Manual," dated 1795, contained information about a "Master Wang of Shanxi." Tang initially believed that this was Wang Zong Yue, but later agreed with historian Xu Zhen that the document was probably based on a text written by Wu Yu Xiang.

9. Exact dates for Chang are not known, though he lived during the Qian Long period (1736–1795) of the Qing dynasty. Xu Zhen conjectures a place for Chang in Wang Zong Yue's lineage. There is no evidence for this.

10. Different versions of this story variously have Jiang Fa teaching Chen Wang Ting (Chen Village ninth generation, 1600–1680) and Chen Chang Xing (Chen Village fourteenth generation, 1771–1853).

11. Qi Ji Guang (1528–1587) is one of China's most renowned military figures, credited with defeating hordes of Japanese marauders in Tai Zhou and Guang Dong.

12. Wen Zee, *Wu Style Tai Chi Chuan,* pp. 14–15.

13. Attaching such importance to the name "Taijiquan" is a common tactic: the Chen system could not have been Taijiquan because it was called something else. By logical extension of this reasoning, Yang Style is also not Taijiquan because it used to be called "Cotton Boxing." Moreover, empty-handed martial arts *(quan)* of any kind could not have existed prior to the Southern Song dynasty because before that time they were called *shou bo.* The term "Taijiquan" was probably not used before about 1854.

14. Zee, p. 16.

15. Ibid., p. 12.

16. According to the *Huaiqing Prefecture Chronicle,* the *Wen County Chronicle,* and the *Anping County Chronicle,* Chen Wang Ting held this post three years before the end of the Ming dynasty, when he led troops against assaulting "bandits."

17. Gu Liuxin, *Chen Style Taijiquan*, p. 3.

18. Ibid., p. 2.

19. Tang did not have access to Qi's complete text, so cited only twenty-five corresponding movements. Later discovery of the complete text revealed four more.

20. T. Dufresne and J. Nguyen, *Taiji Quan*, p. 57.

21. Chen Wang Ting, "Song of the Classic of Boxing," in *Chen Style Taijiquan Second Form*, by Gu Liuxin, p. 300.

22. These parallels are cited in Wile's *T'ai Chi's Ancestors*, pp. 14–15, and in Stanley Henning's excellent review of same in *Journal of Asian Martial Arts*.

23. Chen Xin claims that Chang apprenticed in Chen Village. This cannot be verified.

24. There are two different Taiji styles whose names, while different in Chinese, transliterate to the same Latin spelling (Wu). To distinguish them, they are sometimes called "Big Wu" (from Wu Jian Quan) and "Small Wu" (from Wu Yu Xiang).

25. Quan You originally studied under Lu Chan himself, but he was not of sufficiently high social rank to be listed in the genealogy as a martial-arts brother of the nobility. He was therefore recorded as a student of Ban Hou.

# Chapter 3: **Instruction**

1. The term *ru men* is often translated as "indoor," but this is nonsensical. "One who has entered the door" is better, if rather unwieldy.

# Chapter 4: **Basics**

1. Bagua practitioner Cheng Ting Hua, Taiji practitioner Liu De Guan, and Xingyi practitioners Li Cun Yi and Liu Wei Xiang.

2. Wile, *Lost T'ai Chi Classics*, p. 135.

3. In advanced forms, weight is sometimes committed immediately to the front foot. This issue does not concern us here.

4. The eight basic techniques plus the five phases comprise the so-called "Thirteen Postures" mentioned in Wang Zong Yue's "Treatise."

5. The term *chan si jin* comes from the silk-manufacture process: the cocoon spins and unwinds as the end of the thread is pulled. *Chan si jin* is present in other styles of Taijiquan, but less distinctly than in Chen Style.

6. In sports physiology, a "plyometric" action is one where an eccentric muscle contraction (in which the muscle contracts to shorten a stretch) is followed immediately by a concentric contraction (in which the muscle shortens as it contracts). Modern sports "scientists" are fond of thinking that they invented plyometric training as an optimum method for increasing speed and power, but, as we can see, Chinese martial artists were doing this in an infinitely more sophisticated way hundreds of years ago.

## Chapter 5: **Forms**

1. The double straight-sword is also practiced slowly, but this form was a late addition to the system.

# Bibliography

Adams, Douglas. *Dirk Gently's Holistic Detective Agency*. New York: Pocket Books, 1988.

Chen, Qing Zhou. *Chen Family Taijiquan Martial Arts Compendium* (in Chinese). Beijing: Zhong Hua Publishing, 2002.

Chen, Wang Ting. "Song of the Classic of Boxing." In *Chen Style Taijiquan Second Form: Cannon Fist* (in Chinese), by Gu Liuxin. Rev. ed. 1985. Reprint, Hong Kong: Hai Feng Publishing Co., 1994.

Chen, Wei-Ming. *T'ai Chi Ch'uan Ta Wen: Questions and Answers on T'ai Chi Ch'uan*. Trans. Pang Jeng Lo and Robert W. Smith. Berkeley, CA: North Atlantic Books, 1985.

Chen, Xin. *Illustrated Manual of Chen Family Taijiquan* (in Chinese). 1933. Author's Preface, 1919. Reprint, Hong Kong: Chen Xiang Ji Publishing, 1983.

Draeger, Donn F., and Smith, Robert W. *Comprehensive Asian Fighting Arts*. Tokyo: Kodansha International Ltd., 1980.

Dufresne, T., and Nguyen, J. *Taiji Quan: Art martial ancien de la famille Chen*. Paris: Éditions Budostore, 1994.

Eidam, Klaus. *The True Life of J.S. Bach*. Trans. Hoyt Rogers. New York: Basic Books, 2001.

Fu, Zhongwen. *Mastering Yang Style Taijiquan*. Trans. Louis Swaim. Berkeley, CA: North Atlantic Books, 1999.

Gu, Liuxin. *Chen Style Taijiquan Second Form: Cannon Fist* (in Chinese). Rev. ed. 1985. Reprint, Hong Kong: Hai Feng Publishing Co., 1994.

Gu, Liuxin. "The Origin, Evolution and Development of Shadow Boxing." In *Chen Style Taijiquan*. Comp. Zhaohua Publishing House. Hong Kong: Hai Feng Publishing Co., 1984.

Henning, Stanley. "Academia Encounters the Chinese Martial Arts." *China Review International 6*, no. 2 (1999): 319–32.

Henning, Stanley. "Ignorance, Legend and Taijiquan." *Journal of the Chenstyle Taijiquan Research Association of Hawaii* 2, no. 3 (1994): 4–5.

Henning, Stanley. "The Origin of the Name 'Taijiquan.'" *Taijiquan Journal* 2, no. 1 (2001): 6–7.

Henning, Stanley. Review of *T'ai Chi's Ancestors: The Making of an Internal Martial Art,* by Douglas Wile. *Journal of Asian Martial Arts* 10, no. 1 (2001): 100–103.

Henning, Stanley. "What's the Military Got to Do with Taijiquan? " *Taijiquan Journal* 3, no. 2 (2002): 23–24.

Jou, Tsung Hwa. *The Tao of Tai-chi Chuan: Way to Rejuvenation.* Ed. Shoshana Shapiro. Rev. ed. Piscataway, NJ: Tai Chi Foundation, 1983.

Kang, Gewu. *The Spring and Autumn of Chinese Martial Arts: 5000 Years.* Santa Cruz, CA: Plum Publishing, 1995.

Lee, Bruce. *The Bruce Lee Library.* Ed. John Little. Vol. 2, *The Tao of Gung Fu.* Boston: Charles E. Tuttle Co., 1997.

Liao, Waysun. *T'ai Chi Classics.* 1977. Reprint, Boston: Shambhala Publications, 1990.

Lo, Benjamin Pang Jeng, et al. *The Essence of T'ai Chi Ch'uan: The Literary Tradition.* 1979. Reprint, Berkeley, CA: North Atlantic Books, 1985.

Miller, Dan. "Sun Lu Tang: His Life and Teaching." In *Xing Yi Quan Xue: The Study of Form-Mind Boxing,* by Sun Lu Tang. Trans. Albert Liu. Burbank, CA: Unique Publications, 2000.

People's Physical Culture Publishing. *Complete Book of Taijiquan* (in Chinese). 1988. Reprint, Beijing: People's Physical Culture Publishing, 1994.

Qi, Ji Guang. "Boxing Classic: Essentials for Victory." In *Chen Style Taijiquan Second Form: Cannon Fist* (in Chinese), by Gu Liuxin. Rev. ed. 1985. Reprint, Hong Kong: Hai Feng Publishing Co., 1994. Originally published in Qi Ji Guang, *New Book of Effective Discipline* (ca. 1561, in Chinese).

Smith, Robert W. *Secrets of Shaolin Temple Boxing.* 1964. Reprint, Rutland, VT: Charles E. Tuttle Co., 1984.

Wile, Douglas. *Lost T'ai-chi Classics from the Late Ch'ing Dynasty.* Albany: State Univ. of New York Press, 1996.

Wile, Douglas. *T'ai Chi's Ancestors: The Making of an Internal Martial Art.* New York: Sweet Ch'i Press, 1999.

Wycherley, R.E. *The Stones of Athens.* Princeton: Princeton Univ. Press, 1978.

Zee, Wen. *Wu Style Tai Chi Chuan: Ancient Chinese Way to Health.* Berkeley, CA: North Atlantic Books, 2002.